Breaking the Ice

Breaking the Ice

A Guide to Understanding People from Other Cultures

Second Edition

Daisy Kabagarama
Wichita State University

Allyn and Bacon
Boston • London • Toronto • Sydney • Tokyo • Singapore

To my fellow citizens who dream of a peaceful world;
a world of hope, joy, and tranquillity;
a world of harmony, justice, and truth;
a world that was intended to be.

Contents

Preface

When I wrote the first edition of this book, I was trying out an idea of assembling a text in cross-cultural understanding that would appeal across disciplines, have practical applications and be grounded in theory. I also wanted to invite my readers to examine a world in which tremendous change was taking place, calling us to act in unison, as world citizens. This noble task was accomplished three years ago. The compliments and support that I have received from all corners of the world have been tremendous.

Time has now come to revise the first edition and add some new perspectives. The second edition is intended to offer fresh insight into the world of today, just a few years from the 21st century. This edition is also aimed at creating a new sense of urgency toward addressing major challenges that face humanity today. One such challenge that will be discussed in depth is that of cross-cultural understanding. More discussion topics and exercises will be added to those that were presented in the first edition.

Very new to this edition is a section that focuses on what organizations can do to promote cross-cultural awareness and understanding. In the first edition, the discussion focused primarily on individual encounters. Since the majority of individuals work and spend most of their lives in organizations of all sorts, it's only wise that the discussion also pays attention to this level of analysis.

It is my great hope that this book provides an avenue through which important issues and concepts such as race, ethnicity, diversity, multiculturalism, cultural awareness, cultural understanding and respect can be discussed freely, willingly and happily. Whether one belongs to the majority, dominant culture or the minority one, we all get affected by the tensions that result from a lack of understanding. The debate needs to be engaged in by all. Hopefully this book will facilitate such dialogue. The next century should find us all in a state of readiness and this book is offering its readers a "jump start."

The Dawn of an Era

Yes it's here, that hour of reckoning
Indeed it's here, that hour of recollection
The hour to gather what was lost
The hour to search at whatever cost
To look for that blessed hope
To mend the broken dreams
To plant new seed
Into fertile ground that yields plenty
To learn from the past
Reflect on the present
And dream for the future
It is a new era one cannot run from

Its truth and colors shine bright
It's a new era to stand tall
It's a new era to answer the call
It's a new era to reconnect
It's a new era to project
The era like no other
Bringing us together

(Kabagarama, 1996)

ACKNOWLEDGMENTS

Engaging in a writing adventure can sometimes be a lonesome and anxiety-arousing undertaking. Feelings of lonesomeness arise because the author alone has the image of what needs to be shared. The task lies in the ability to convey such an image effectively to an audience who may have a feel for the same or none at all. Anxiety sets in when the author realizes that many eyes are going to read what has been written. "Will they understand what I'm trying to say?" is a constant question in the author's mind. The good news is that often some individuals run to the rescue of the author and restore her/him to a level of comfort and assurance that enables the project to be completed.

One of the individuals that I'm very much indebted to is Karen Hanson of Allyn and Bacon. I often feel that she is not only an editor, but a mentor. Through her gentle probing, she has enabled me to remain focused and to produce the best results. She has often understood what I had to say, before I fully articulated it. I also very much appreciate the support which I have received from the whole staff of Allyn and Bacon. Another person that I am greatly indebted to is Dr. Charlotte Bruner, who has nurtured my writing and brought it to this level. Her confidence in me has enabled me to soar to great heights. I often think that she knows where I'm coming from and where I'm going in my professional life. She appreciates my ability to blend fine arts with the social sciences, knowing that the two enrich each other.

Thanks to the great teachers that I encountered at various levels of my education. Special thanks go to Professor Mary Kihl of Arizona State University and Professor Charles L. Mulford of Iowa State University. Their understanding, support and encouragement have provided me a strong sense of security, thereby saving me from professional loneliness and isolation. I am always confident that I can count on them in time of need.

My sincere appreciation goes to my colleagues at Wichita State University for their support. Although I've been here for a short while, I feel welcome and appreciated. Many have paid a listening ear in time of need. They have also provided an audience with whom to share ideas.

Many thanks go to my students who believe in me, offer new challenges and provide me with fresh new ideas. Their appreciation of my work gives me courage to carry on. I always boast, with confidence, that if no one else reads my work, my wonderful students will. I also trust their opinions, which are often genuine and helpful.

My writing project would not have been so well-done without the help of my most able typist, Cindy Penner. Besides her excellent work skills, she has such a gentle approach to tasks that makes me feel at ease. I also know I can always depend on her to accomplish the task in a timely manner. She also made very kind remarks with regard to how much she was enjoying the discussion in the book.

Last but not least, special thanks go to my family. Before writing this section of the book, I had a long conversation with my mother who came all the way from Uganda, to the U.S. to visit us, after twelve years of separation. Her courage, inspiration and sense of adventure are very well exhibited in my work. I am also very much indebted to my maternal grandmother who passed on to me her great wisdom. She also taught me at an early age, how to care for others. Thanks to my husband and children whose support and encouragement constantly provide me "the wind beneath my wing." My husband read through the entire text and remarked, "It is perfect."

Friends We All Need

Once in a while, we all need friends
Those few on whom life depends
Friends with encouraging words
Friends with soothing tongues
Friends with insightful minds
Gently correcting
Wisely guiding
Generously giving
Freely sharing
All that they have
With dignity and love

(Kabagarama, 1996)

Breaking the Ice

Introduction

"We have learned the lesson that our blemishes speak of what all humanity should not do. We understand fully that our glories point to the heights of what human genius can achieve."[1]—Nelson Mandela, May 24, 1994

We are living in a rapidly-changing world. Within the past decade, major political changes have occurred around the world, thereby creating new power relations. With the falling of the South African apartheid system, the crumbling of the Berlin Wall and the collapse of the Soviet Union, there are obvious new faces on the political scene. On the economic front, new giants such as those of the Pacific Rim have emerged and so have new trade relationships such as NAFTA (North American Free Trade Agreement). Other bilateral and multilateral trading relations, perhaps not so well publicized are in existence in different parts of the world. With these new arrangements, there is hope that through cooperation, people from different corners of the world can work together to improve the human condition.

On the unattractive side, major world catastrophes that threaten our existence do occur every day. The AIDS epidemic, hunger, wars such as the ones experienced in Bosnia, Rwanda and Somalia and numerous examples of racial, ethnic and religious conflict are a constant reminder that tremendous tension exists. If causes of such tension are not thoroughly and honestly examined and much effort devoted toward finding solutions, discomfort and pain could easily be carried into the 21st century. With specific reference to the United States, major problems confront our very own backyards. Violent crime, drug abuse, teenage pregnancies are on the rise while education standards, particularly those in inner city schools continue to fall. All these problems are occurring while families are highly unstable and children are committing crime at an increasingly young age. Well, what does this discussion have to do with this book? The simple answer is that in order to make an attempt at addressing these problems and many others, people have to have a common ground. Cultural differences create barriers among us, sometimes so strong, that crossing them to solve our common problems seems to be an impossible task. The well-renowned Üner Kirdar expresses the following view:

> *These global issues call for joint policy action that goes beyond the short-term interests of national states with different levels of development and different political regimen. They are indeed the global challenges of the international community, ranging from the economic requirements of finance, trade, and monetary exchanges to the social needs for food, health, education and employment, from energy to*

I

ecology, from information to new discoveries in genetics and biotechnology. Most of these challenges are dealt with not only through the framework of national states or by a limited group of states, but also at sectoral levels. Many of the crucial problems affecting the well-being of a large segment of humanity today can no longer be solved by strictly national fragmented efforts. The rate of change in and the growth of the dimensions of these types of issues transcend the ability of individual states, self-determined national policies and classically defined sectoral disciplines![1]

One World

It's one world
My friend, it's one world
Our barriers
Our fears
Have put us apart
While we don't have to part
It's one world
My friend, it's one world
Look at the valleys
And look at the hills
Picture the creatures
And picture the seas
It's one world
My friend, it's one world
Listen to the birds
And listen to their cries
Visit the animals
Listen to their songs
It's one world
My friend, it's one world
When all
In all
We stumble
And fall
We see
And feel
That strife
And faith
Are part of one world

(Kabagarama, 1993)

NEED FOR GLOBAL EDUCATION

The rapid changes in the world call for educational institutions to seize the opportunity to equip students with skills that will enable them to deal effectively with people from diverse backgrounds. Education has always been and continues to be an avenue for change. Major world breakthroughs in medicine, technology, the arts, and other areas have been facilitated by educational institutions. Even in the most simple society, education is highly valued as the medium through which values are inculcated in succeeding generations.

As we move into the era of globalization, educators need to teach students survival techniques in the global village. Brown[2] strongly argues that social change occurs when people change the way they perceive some elements constituting their world. He goes on to say that change can be spurred by a charismatic leader, a dramatic event, or a gradual awakening through education. People cross a "perceptual threshold" and begin seeing some aspects of their world in a new light.

In order to avoid applying a "band-aid" approach to global education, we must provide a philosophical base that fosters a belief in equity for all human beings. This philosophy needs to emphasize that all people, at any level of technology or social development, have the capacity to contribute to the good of the world if given a chance. An education grounded in this type of reasoning would free learners from fear of the unknown.

Besides being an avenue to fostering world peace, global education helps people to carry out day-to-day transactions. By showing them how entangled their lives are in the world socioeconomic and geopolitical context, such an education prepares the students to make informed choices. They also develop skills and attitudes for effectively living in a world possessing limited natural resources, ethnic diversity, and characterized by interdependence. Research shows that people who have been exposed to other cultures have an advantage in handling conflict and problem-solving.[3]

Gang,[4] a strong believer in education, posits that if we are able to see the historical turning point at which we stand, we can then move deliberately and consciously to influence our direction. Speaking in favor of global education, Muller,[5] a retired assistant secretary-general of the United Nations, states the following:

> *We must give a global vision to all the world's children, teach them about the miracle and sanctity of life, the necessity for love for our planet, for our great human family, for the heavens and for the creator of all these marvels. We must teach them rules of good behavior toward our global home and all our human sisters and brothers, so as to ensure peace, justice and happiness for all.*

DISCUSSION TOPIC

Thoroughly discuss five major problems confronting the world today. Suggest solutions to those problems.

ENDNOTES

1. Nelson Mandela, *Ebony* (August 1994).
2. Üner Kirdar, *Change: Threat or Opportunity?* (New York: United Nations Publications, 1992).
3. Lester Brown, *State of the World: 1989* (New York: W.W. Norton Company, Inc., 1989).
4. Robert E. Freeman, *Promising Practices in Global Education* (New York: National Council on Foreign Language and International Studies, 1986).
5. Philip S. Gang, *Rethinking Education* (Atlanta: Dagaz Press, 1989).
6. R. Muller, *New Genesis* (New York: Doubleday and Company, 1982), 59.

A Changing World

"I am a citizen, not of Athens or Greece, but
of the world." —SOCRATES

Available data and evidence provided by recent world events point in the direction of a changing world. Changes permeate all areas of human activity including population, business, technology, work relations, and roles of women.

POPULATION

At the beginning of the 1970s, the world population was about 3.5 billion people, which increased to 4 billion by 1974. With approximately 83 million people added every year, it did not take long to reach the 5 billion mark in July of 1987. There are no signs indicating that population growth will slow down markedly in the near future. In fact, it is projected to reach 6.3 billion by the year 2000 (see Table 1.1).[1] Population distribution and the allocation of resources among the world's people will be issues of great concern at international meetings. Even though the less industrialized countries occupy 49% of the world's land and contain about 3/4 of its population, their share of world resources is very meager. This condition is presented in Table 1.2.[2] Many of these countries, particularly those in Africa, were colonies of European countries. After gaining their independence, many were left with systems of education, politics and economics that were alien to their traditional methods of conducting business. This mismatch of values, combined with world inflation, unequal terms of trade in the global economy, colonial exploitation and political instability has created a situation where most of these countries are stagnant in their growth process.

The rest of the world cannot afford to ignore the poor countries. They are major players in world economic and political affairs. They produce and consume products, contribute ideas to international politics and are major players in the peace process. Their plea for equity, justice and human rights cannot be ignored or paid lip service in an era of

TABLE 1.1 **Estimated and Projected Population Size by Region, 1950–2025**

Region	Population (millions)				
	1950	1970	1990	2000	2025
World Total	2,516	3,698	5,292	6,261	8,504
Industrialized countries	832	1,049	1,207	1,264	1,354
Developing countries	1,684	2,649	4,086	4,997	7,150
Africa	222	363	642	867	1,597
North America	166	226	276	295	332
Latin America	166	286	448	538	757
Asia	1,377	2,102	3,113	3,713	4,912
Europe	393	460	498	510	515
Oceania	13	19	26	30	38
U.S.S.R.*	180	243	289	308	352

Source: United Nations Population Division, World Population Prospects 1990 (United Nations, New York 1991), pp. 226-233, 244-245, 252-255, 264-265, 274-275, and 582-583.
*The former U.S.S.R. is currently under different subdivisions.

global interdependence. Concerns over issues such as pollution, drug abuse, natural resource depletion, racism, sexism, ethnic violence, disease and poverty will not be meaningful unless all people, whether rich or poor, are given an equal hearing. The world inflation of the 1970s and the current AIDS epidemic are proof to the fact that indeed people share the same world. They either flourish or perish together.

BUSINESS

The era of isolationism in business ventures is over. Strong regional centers are replacing economic entities built around individual nations. The concept of "comparative advantage" is going to be more evident in the future than ever before. Naisbitt and Aburdene[3] remark that the new era of globalization has begun and that there is an international call to environmentalism. They add that among nations, the desire for economic cooperation is stronger than the urge for military adventure.

Since the 1960s, U.S. multinational corporations have moved several manufacturing operations abroad. By the 1980s, they were manufacturing and selling nearly three times as much in foreign countries as they made and exported from the United States. General Electric, for example, produces half a billion dollars worth of cassette recorders, microwave ovens, room air conditioners, and telephones in Asian nations every year. Close examination of economic realities shows that during the 1950s the United States made over 80 percent of the world's automobiles. This figure has come down to a little over 20 percent presently. While only 50 percent of U.S. industries faced foreign competition four decades ago, currently 75 percent are under constant pressure to keep up with foreign op-

TABLE I.I *continued*

Region	Percent Share of World Population				
	1950	1970	1990	2000	2025
World Total	100.0	100.0	100.0	100.0	100.0
Industrialized countries	33.1	28.4	22.8	20.2	15.9
Developing countries	66.9	71.6	77.2	79.8	84.1
Africa	8.8	9.8	12.1	13.8	18.8
North America	6.6	6.1	5.2	4.7	3.9
Latin America	6.6	7.7	8.5	8.6	8.9
Asia	54.7	56.8	58.8	59.3	57.8
Europe	15.6	12.4	9.4	8.1	6.1
Oceania	0.5	0.5	0.5	0.5	0.4
U.S.S.R.*	7.2	6.6	5.5	4.9	4.1

erations. The banking situation has also changed dramatically, with the Japanese managing the world's ten largest banks.[4]

TECHNOLOGY

Technology has not only taken human beings to the moon but has also facilitated greater contact between people from different cultures. At the pressing of a button, for example, one can easily transact business between New York and any other major city in the world. Tremendous volumes of information can be shared through computers. The common stock market is proof that even private affairs such as those regarding monetary resources are shared worldwide. Our economic behavior is not only monitored by family members and those with whom we share cultural values, but by those foreign to us as well. With sophisticated banking methods and the use of credit cards, it is no longer necessary for people to carry large sums of currency from country to country. In addition, satellites which enable people to communicate with each other across vast water and land masses have made it possible for people to share and process information much faster than was possible previously. Sophisticated communication technology such as the Internet is allowing people to accomplish more tasks. On the negative side, such communication technology facilitates the transfer of social problems such as child pornography.

Freedom to travel has also been enhanced. People travel from one region of the world to another for different reasons. While some do so for cultural, economic and educational exchanges, others travel as tourists seeking adventure and leisure. There are others who leave their places of birth permanently to settle elsewhere, fleeing political persecution or poverty. The United States has historically accepted people from other nations based on all the reasons mentioned above. Table 1.3[5] shows the types of people who entered the nation, according to the data compiled in 1993.

TABLE I.2 **Levels of Income in the Three Worlds**

Country	Per Capital Income[a]
First World	
Switzerland	$35,590
Japan	27,300
United States	22,550
Canada	20,840
United Kingdom	17,400
Second World	
Soviet Union*	8,639
Czechoslovakia	6,914
Poland	4,185
Third World	
China	1,327
El Salvador	1,075
India	303
Nigeria	242
Mozambique	74
Newly Industrializing Countries	
Taiwan	9,068
South Korea	6,430
Mexico	3,051
Brazil	2,601

Source: Anthony Giddens, 1996: p. 51.

[a]Per capita income is the value of all goods and services produced in the economy divided by the population.
*The former Soviet Union is currently under different subdivisions.

IMMIGRATION

DeVita[6] notes that three words describe the U.S. population in the mid-1990s; large, diverse and growing. While some of the increase is from child-bearing in the native population, a large segment can be attributed to immigration. Since the 1950s, the number of immigrants to the United States has steadily been rising. Currently, most of these come from Latin American and Asian countries. This offers a sharp contrast to the 1960s period when the largest number of immigrants came from Europe and Canada.[7]

A huge wave of immigrants entered the country in the late 1980s and early 1990s, peaking in 1990 when a record number of 1.8 million were legally admitted. Others had lived in the country, illegally until the 1986 Immigration Reform and Control Act (IRCA) granted them legal status. When emigration is taken into account, about 1 million people are added to the U.S. population every year.[8]

While the number of European immigrants to the United States has declined over the years, migration from other regions has steadily increased, bringing in cultures that are

TABLE I.3 Entrants to the United States, 1993

Category	Numbers (in thousands)	Percent
Immigrants, Refugees and Asylees	904	100
IRCA* legalizations	24	3
Non-IRCA immigrants	880	97
Immediate relatives of U.S. citizens	255	28
Other family based	227	25
Employment based	147	16
Other	124	14
Refugees and asylees	127	14
Nonimmigrants	21,447	100
Tourists	16,900	79
Business visitors	2,962	14
Temporary workers	165	1
Students	257	1
Other	1,163	5
Unauthorized immigrants		
Estimated entries	1,500 to 2,500	
Estimated illegal settlers	300	

Source: INS, 1993 Statistical Yearbook
*IRCA "Immigration Reform Control Act of 1986"

distinctly different from the traditional Euro-American culture. The excerpt below illustrates this complex situation:

> The American ethnic mosaic is being fundamentally altered; ethnicity itself is being redefined, its new images redefined in the popular media and reflected in myriad and often surprising ways. Immigrants from a score of nationalities are told that they are all 'Hispanics,' while far more diverse groups—from India and Laos, China and the Philippines—are lumped together as 'Asians.' There are foreign-born mayors of large American cities, first-generation millionaires who speak broken English, a proliferation of sweatshops exploiting immigrant labor in an expanding informal economy, and new myths that purport to 'explain' the success or failure of different ethnic groups. Along 'Calle Ocho' in Miami's Little Havana, shops post signs to reassure potential customers that they'll find 'English spoken here,' while Koreatown retailers in Los Angeles display 'Se habla espanol' signs next to their own Hangul script, a businesslike acknowledgment that the largest Mexican and Salvadoran communities in the world outside of Mexico and El Salvador are located there. In Brooklyn, along Brighton Beach Avenue ('Little Odessa'), signs written in Cyrillic letters by new Soviet immigrants have replaced old English and

Yiddish signs. In Houston, the auxiliary bishop is a Cuban-born Jesuit who speaks fluent Vietnamese—an overflow [crowd] of 6,000 faithful attended his recent ordination, and he addressed them in three languages—and the best Cuban cafe is run by Koreans. In a Farsi-language Iranian immigrant monthly in Los Angeles, Rah-E-Zendegi, next to announcements for 'Business English' classes, a classified ad offers for sale a $20 million square block on Boston's Commonwealth Avenue, and other ads deal with tax shelters, mergers, and acquisitions. In Santa Barbara, a preliterate Hmong woman from the Laotian highlands, recently converted to Christianity, asked her pastor if she could enter heaven without knowing how to read; while in Chattanooga, Tennessee, a twelve-year-old Cambodian refugee, Linn Yann, placed second in a regional spelling bee (she missed on 'enchilada'). At the Massachusetts Institute of Technology, Tue Hguyen, a twenty-six-year-old Vietnamese boat refugee, set an MIT record in 1988 by earning his seventh advanced degree, a doctorate in nuclear engineering, just nine years after arriving in the United States—and landed a job at IBM designing technology for the manufacture of semiconductors.[9]

The topic of immigration often raises strong emotions. Some blame immigrants, especially those with poor education, for population growth and congestion, keeping wages low, retarding the general modernization process, dependence on public assistance and increasing ethnic tension. On the opposite side of the coin are arguments in support of immigration. It is a test to the American democracy because often, the immigrants are escaping from political and socioeconomic oppression. Others view immigrants as a resource in enriching the cultural flavor of the nation. As former president J. F. Kennedy once noted, "Everywhere immigrants have enriched and strengthened the fabric of American Life."[10] Another argument in favor is that immigrants keep the economy healthy by taking on jobs that would otherwise be considered undesirable by the native-born workers. Those immigrants with high education and skill levels bring new knowledge to the society and contribute to economic development. Whatever side of the debate one may appear to be, the issue of immigration cannot be taken lightly.

Martin and Midgley suggest that immigrants have their greatest demographic impact at the state and local levels. They, for example, visit local health facilities and attend schools. Because most immigrants tend to be of child-bearing age, their impact is felt more in schools than work places. In 1990, for example, in the State of California, although the Hispanics, Asians and other minorities accounted for less than 30% of the state's population, they made up more than half of the elementary school population.[11] This poses a major challenge to an education system that is predominantly monoethnic. In order for such students to succeed, changes need to occur at all levels. Teachers, administrators and staff need cultural education and skills to function effectively in a multicultural setting. Students, too, need to be taught skills to function effectively in a multicultural environment.

TABLE 1.4 Racial and Ethnic Populations in the United States, 1990

Race or Ethnicity	Population	Percentage of Total Population
African origin	29,986,000	12.1
Hispanic origin[a]	22,354,000	9.0
Mexican	13,496,000	5.4
Puerto Rican	2,728,000	1.1
Cuban	1,044,000	0.4
Other Hispanic	5,086,000	2.0
Asian or Pacific Island origin	7,274,000	2.9
Chinese	1,645,000	0.7
Filipino	1,407,000	0.6
Japanese	848,000	0.3
Korean	799,000	0.3
Vietnamese	615,000	0.2
Hawaiian	211,000	0.1
Samoan	63,000	<[b]
Guamanian	49,000	<
Other Asian or Pacific Island	822,000	0.3
Native American	1,959,000	0.8
American Indian	1,878,000	0.8
Eskimo	57,000	<
Aleut	24,000	<
European origin	199,686,000	80.3

Source: U.S. Bureau of the Census, 1992.

[a]People of Hispanic origin can be of any race.

[b]Indicates less than 1/20 of 1 percent.

THE U.S. CULTURAL MIX

The U.S. blending of cultures is a phenomenon that is noticed, worldwide. O'Hare, for example, notes: "To the rest of the world, the United States is a grand and daring experiment. No country has every succeeded in blending so many people of different races and different cultures."[12] Right from its founding, the U.S. has always been a nation of many cultures. Table 1.4[13] presents the 1990 racial and ethnic data.

Future trends show increasing cultural diversity in the U.S., thereby changing the face of the whole nation.. The shift is from a society predominantly comprised of individuals of European ancestry to one of diverse racial and ethnic groups. Scholars predict that by the year 2050, the nation will be "majority-minority," in which no one racial or ethnic group will predominate! This emerging trend is presented in Table 1.5[14] and Figure 1.1.[15]

TABLE 1.5 Composition of U.S. Population (1995 and 2020)

Group	1995	2020
Blacks	12%	13%
Hispanics	10%	16%
Non-hispanic whites	74%	64%
Asians	3%	6%
Native Americans	1%	1%

Source: U.S. Bureau of the Census, 1993.

The number of foreign-born permanent residents and citizens is very substantial. Their impact is felt more in some states and cities than others. Tables 1.6[16] and 1.7[17] present data to illustrate this phenomenon.

Another phenomenon that is altering the face of the U.S. society is the changing age structure, commonly referred to as the "graying of America." The median age in 1994 was 34 years, up from 30 years in 1980. As the baby boomers (those born between 1946 and 1964) age, the overall society will look older, since currently, one in three members of the population belongs to this group. In 1994, about 33 million Americans were 65 years of age and over. By year 2030, the number is expected to more than double to 70 million. The ratio of the elderly to children is also changing. Whereas in 1994, the number of children was more than twice that of the adults, by year 2030, children are expected

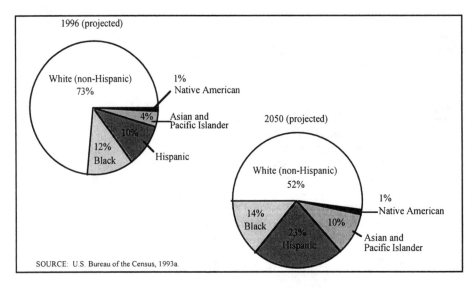

FIGURE 1.1 **The Changing Face of America: Population in the United States by Race and Ethnicity**

TABLE 1.6 U.S.-Born and Foreign-Born Population by Race/Ethnicity in Selected States, 1990

State	Total (1,000s)	Race White	Black	Asian (percent)	Other[a]	Hispanic Origin[b] (percent)
U.S.-Born	228,943	83	13	1	4	6
Foreign-Born	19,767	51	7	23	19	40
California	6,459	40	2	29	29	53
New York	2,852	48	23	19	10	26
Florida	1,663	73	14	6	7	55
Texas	1,524	49	3	15	33	71
New Jersey	967	60	10	21	9	30
Illinois	952	54	3	21	22	38

Source: U.S. Bureau of the Census, 1990 Census.

[a]Includes American Indians, Aleuts, and Eskimos—who accounted for 1 percent of the native-born population and less than 0.5 percent of the foreign-born population in these states. Category also includes persons reporting mixed race and those not specifying race.

[b]Persons of Hispanic origin may be of any race.

to outnumber the elderly by only 15%.[18] The elderly present unique challenges, especially in a society that is youth-oriented. Besides obvious health needs that come about as a result of old age, there are also unique social, psychological and emotional needs that the elderly pose to the society. Often, such needs are so outstanding and unique, while compared to those of the rest of the population that the elderly might be looked at as a distinct cultural group.

The diversity challenge need not be threatening. If properly harnessed, the rewards that come from a plurality of perspectives enriches the knowledge base and moves the society forward. However, if suppressed and not appropriately handled, diversity could breed conflict, animosity, hostility and violence. Speaking from a global perspective, O'Hare reiterates:

> It is to our advantage to view the growing diversity in the U.S. population in an international context because the rise of the global economy is bringing countries of the world closer together . . . . If Americans so choose, our increasing multicultural population can enhance our ability to serve the global marketplace. America's racial and ethnic minorities can help American businesses understand the needs and preferences of people in other countries.[19]

TABLE 1.7 States with 350,000 or More Foreign-Born Residents, 1990

U.S./State	Foreign-born population (1'000s)	Percent of foreign-born in state	Foreign-born as percent of U.S./state population
Total U.S.	19,767	100	8
California	6,459	33	22
New York	2,852	14	16
Florida	1,663	8	13
Texas	1,524	8	9
New Jersey	967	5	13
Illinois	952	5	8
Massachusetts	574	3	10
Pennsylvania	369	2	3
Michigan	355	2	4
All other states	4,052	20	3

Source: U.S. Bureau of the Census, 1990 CPH-L-121 and 1990 CPH-L-134.

Discussion Topic

What are the benefits and challenges of living in a culturally-diverse society?

CHANGING WORK RELATIONS AND THE ROLE OF WOMEN

Work organizations are increasingly being faced with the challenge of coping with a changing environment in which cultural diversity is a major force to reckon with. Immigrants, native-born racial and ethnic minorities, who are on the rise, bring with them cultural patterns that are different and often in conflict with those of the majority Caucasian population. Women, who in many ways have a world view that is different from that of males, are entering the labor force and assuming managerial positions at a very rapid rate. Based on current trends, scholars predict that by the year 2000, women will make up 47% of America's workers. Minorities and immigrants will hold 26% of the jobs. This figure will be up from 22% in 1990. Similar predictions reveal that between now and the end of the century, 85% of the new entrants into the labor force will be minorities, women, and immigrants, while native-born white males will make up only 15%.[20]

These changes call for adjustments in managerial style and work relations. Managers who once had a homogeneous group of employees are now facing minorities who may not only speak a different language, but are motivated differently. It is also common to find minorities in managerial positions, as shown by over one million African-American managers and professionals.[21] Not only do these numbers alter the traditional power structure, but they require a new style of communication. A study by the U.S. Merit System Protection Board, for example, observed that 42 percent of the women who worked for the federal government reported that they had been sexually harassed either verbally or physically.[22]

Since the 1930s, female labor force participation rates have grown steadily and continue to do so. Women introduce a different cultural element to the labor force. As more of them hold managerial positions, for example, individuals who are not used to having female bosses have to adjust. Further, as more women of child-bearing age go to work, issues of childcare will need to be given high priority in business meetings. In addition to such changes, people have to get used to seeing informal relationships between males and females which are not necessarily "romantic." Just as men have had to form networks in order to learn the rules of operating business from informal settings, more and more women will have to do the same with colleagues, both females and males. Male-dominated clubs will need to open their doors to women.

Roles of women are changing worldwide. As they acquire higher education, their leadership ability improves. There are, for example, women serving their governments in various capacities including heads of state, cabinet ministers, military advisors, and leaders in different professions and business enterprises. As women become more wealthy and educated, they will directly influence choices on the international scene. They are, for example, influencing clothing fashions, television programs, and children's products. Their influence on the scientific, intellectual, and political communities is steadily rising.

All these changes in work relations mean that people at all levels of influence need to prepare themselves to deal with new cultures. Even when we least expect to run into a stranger, there will always be one. They are buyers of products, consumers and distributors of information, professionals, coworkers or classmates, and can prove to be very dependable friends, if handled in a proper manner. Whatever their role might be, they have a lot to contribute to society both at the micro- and macrosociological levels. Keffler summarizes the changes thus:

> *Demographic shifts, the mounting pace of global competition, political upheaval in major world markets, cultural diversity, ever-changing technology and ever-changing product life cycles, all these factors are very real. And whether you see them as negative or positive, they require very different managerial behaviors and skills from those that currently prevail.*[23]

DISCUSSION TOPICS

1. Discuss various ways in which technology has facilitated closer contact between different peoples of the world.
2. What role will the U.N. play in the 21st century?
3. Discuss ways in which scarce world resources can be equitably distributed worldwide.

EXERCISES

1. Try to envision the world in the year 2020.

a. What dominant groups can you identify and what makes them dominant?
b. What less dominant groups can you identify and what makes them less dominant?
c. Make a list of contributions by the dominant groups to the world.
d. Make a list of contributions by the less dominant groups to the world.
2. Get into small groups of four to five people. Discuss major changes that are occurring in your country and the whole world. After 15-20 minutes of discussion, get back to the large group and share your ideas. Try to answer the following questions:
a. How are these changes likely to affect me as an individual?
b. How are these changes likely to affect my nation?
c. How are these changes likely to affect the whole world?
3. Look around your home or room, starting with the clothes that you are wearing. For each item that you see, write down the name of the country where it was made and share your list with other group members.

ENDNOTES

1. United Nations Population Division, *World Population Prospects* (New York: United Nations, 1991).
2. Anthony Giddens, *Introduction to Sociology* (New York: W. W. Norton & Company, 1996), 51.
3. John Naisbitt and Patricia Aburdene, *Megatrends 2000* (New York: William Morrow and Company, Inc., 1990).
4. Mortimer B. Zuckerman, "What Should Make Bush Run Now" (*U.S. News and World Report*, 1989), 70–71.
5. U.S. Immigration and Naturalization Service (Washington, D.C.: Statistical Yearbook, 1993).
6. Carol Devita, *The United States at Mid-Decade* (Washington, D.C.: Population Bulletin, vol. 50, no. 4, 1996), 2.
7. Philip Martin and Elizabeth Midgley, *Immigration to the United States: Journey to an Uncertain Destination* (Washington, D.C.: Population Bulletin, vol. 49, no. 2, 1994).
8. Ibid.
9. Rubén G. Rumbaut, "Passages to America: Perspectives on the New Immigration" *America at Century's End*, ed. Alan Wolfe (Berkeley: University of California Press), 209-210.
10. John F. Kennedy, *A Nation of Immigrants* (New York: Harper and Row, 1964), 3.
11. Martin and Midgley, p. 5.
12. William P. O'Hare, *America's Minorities—The Demographics of Diversity* (Washington, D.C.: Population Bulletin, vol. 47, no. 4, 1994), 4.
13. U.S. Bureau of the Census, *Statistical Abstract of the United States* (Washington, D.C.: Government Printing Office, 1992).
14. U.S. Bureau of the Census, *Population Projections of the United States by Age, Sex and Hispanic Origin: 1993 to 2050* (Washington, D.C.: Government Printing Office, 1993).
15. Anthony Giddens, p. 202.

16. U.S. Bureau of the Census (Washington, D.C.: Census, 1990).
17. U.S. Bureau of the Census (Washington, D.C.: Census, 1990).
18. DeVita, pp. 11–12.
19. William P. O'Hare, p. 4.
20. Bureau of the United States Labor Statistics (Washington, D.C.: 1994).
21. *Time*, 1 March 1989, 67.
22. *U.S. News and World Report*, 1 August 1988, 50.
23. Jean B. Keffler, "Managing Changing Organizations: Don't Stop Communicating" (Minneapolis: Paper delivered at the National Assessment Conference, 1991).

▶ 2

Culture: The Molder of Human Behavior

The term *culture*, although usually taken for granted, has been defined in many ways. Howard defines it as the customary manner in which human groups learn to organize their behavior and thought in relationship to their environment.[1] Haviland calls it a set of rules or standards shared by members of a society which when acted upon by the members, produces behavior that falls within a range that members consider proper and acceptable.[2]

I define culture as the way of life of a group of people. Commonly, people who share a culture are of the same racial and/or ethnic backgrounds and live within geographical proximity. However, it is also possible for people of different racial and/or ethnic backgrounds who are distant geographically to share a culture.

From birth to death, people are constantly faced with cultural messages which may make them feel good or bad about themselves. Good feelings usually arise when the cultural expectations blend well with demands from the environment. Among the majority of Africans, Japanese, and many Latin American cultures, for example, it is polite not to look elders or people of authority in the eye. This is in contradiction with most western cultures where eye contact is a sign of good manners and honesty. A person from a culture that considers eye contact with an authority figure wrong would be at a loss on visiting a culture that contradicts this norm. A good gesture becomes bad and insulting to the host culture,thereby arousing feelings of insecurity, guilt and anxiety.

Names can also be a cause of confusion between people of different cultures. The poem below illustrates the frustration that can arise if one's name does not fit into a certain cultural context.

Call Me Jim

They doubt my name
I doubt my name

18

Yes, it's true
I'm not free
I want to belong
But not for long
Will I inherit
What I cherish
The name of Jim
Yet in my dream
It's only a wish
And not the truth
Yes, I'm Jim
But deep within
The name is TIMI

(Kabagarama, 1993)

The poem demonstrates this individual's feelings of ambivalence. He may have changed his name to fit in a new culture, but has regrets from deep within. It is possible that in his own culture, Timi had a particular meaning that resonated well within that environment. In the new culture, that name may have sounded clumsy, confusing, and probably difficult to pronounce. In an attempt to lessen his frustration, he took on the new name, which sounds like a smart thing to do, yet it has left a deep hole within him. The main reason for this state is that the name Timi was embedded in a cultural context. It is not only a name but a symbol of so many other things. It could, for example, be representative of relatives who meant a great deal to him. Although Jim sounds nice and easy to the listener's ear, it is devoid of cultural flavor and therefore meaningless to the person who is supposed to own it.

COMPONENTS OF CULTURE

Culture has two major components: the *material* and *nonmaterial*. While the former refers to tangible items such as cars, watches, television sets, hoes and houses, the latter is comprised of intangible elements such as values and beliefs. Both the material and nonmaterial components of culture play a major role in influencing people's perceptions of reality, thought and behavior patterns. Although we tend to take material things for granted and might sometimes assume that others like what we like, this may lead to false assumptions. I often tell my students how I appreciate machines such as microwave ovens, washers and dryers. I like them because they save time. However, I often wonder how waves can cook my food properly! I long to have a charcoal stove or firewood so that I can actually see what is happening to my food. I also do not sometimes like to think of what washers do to my clothes. The fact that they are twisted, pounded and turned makes me feel sorry for them. Although I have very well adapted to the convenient life of machines, sometimes I long for the life that I lived as I was growing up. I miss carrying water and firewood on my head and a baby on my back instead of baskets and strollers.

The nonmaterial aspect of culture is very complex simply because it is not tangible. It is very pervasive and affects our daily lives. While we can see and touch cars, washers, watches and buildings, to name a few examples, values, aspirations and emotions are hidden from the naked eye. How do we judge whether someone is beautiful, polite, educated, elegant, or spiritual? Judgment is based on cultural cues that were acquired during the socialization process. Having been socialized to believe that being excessively skinny is a sign of poor health, I find it hard to offer a compliment to someone based on being skinny. Even after living in a society that is youth-oriented for fourteen years, I still revere the elderly because I was socialized to believe that with age comes beauty, dignity and wisdom, as the poem below illustrates.

Old and Gray

When I'm old and gray, notice my presence
When I'm old and gray, acknowledge my wisdom
When I'm old and gray, feel my power
Power that comes from on high
Power that comes with experience
Power that comes with knowledge

When I'm old and gray, treat me with dignity
When I'm old and gray, treat me with kindness
When I'm old and gray, treat me with love
For this is a blessing to the land
Empowering the young with wisdom
Giving strength and courage to the middle-aged
Instilling peace and comfort to the old

When I'm old and gray, listen to my words
When I'm old and gray, seek my prayer
When I'm old and gray, search for my blessing
When I'm old and gray, invoke my laughter
The laughter that rings the bell
The laughter polished with the times
The laughter that sounds a warning
The laughter that is simple and genuine

When I'm old and gray, hold my hand
When I'm old and gray, guide my step
When I'm old and gray, feel my pulse
When I'm old and gray, listen to my song
With age comes wisdom
With age comes courage
With age comes strength
With age comes peace
Making way for the young of today

(Kabagarama, 1996)

The nonmaterial component of culture can be illustrated by the following examples: values, norms, beliefs, emotions, attitudes, aspirations, laws and symbols (see Figure 2.1)

The arrows in Figure 2.1 point in both directions suggesting that culture shapes values, norms, emotions, beliefs, attitudes, aspirations, symbols, laws, perceptions and material possessions. In turn, these impact culture, which means that cultures are dynamic, always undergoing tremendous change. As individual and group qualities change either due to the internal process of growth and maturation or contact with outside groups, cultures also change. It is often possible to experience a case of culture lag where material components of a certain culture have changed, but the nonmaterial aspect lags behind. Computers and microwave ovens can be used to illustrate this point. While such items are in abundant supply, most people, especially those of the older generation, do not easily welcome the idea of using them. These people need to reach a level of comfort whereby the items are perceived to be less threatening. Such a level comes about with knowledge acquisition and practice.

Values that characterize what is desirable are a significant part of culture. Very often, values of one cultural group may be in conflict with those of another. While individualism, competition and winning are core values of U.S. society, East Asian societies of China, Korea and Japan that are deeply rooted in Confucianism put paramount emphasis on proper social relationships and their maintenance. Emphasis on social relationships in Asia and on the individual in the United States produces different patterns of interpersonal

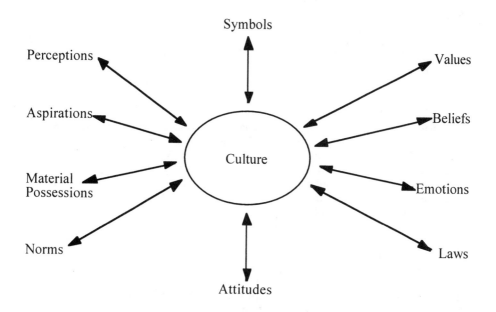

FIGURE 2.1 **The Many Facets of Culture**

and management styles. While the former are mostly preoccupied with personalized, interdependent relationships among employees, the latter spend a great deal of time focusing on equality, fairness and justice issues.[3]

The value placed on time by the U.S. people, particularly those of Northern European descent, has often caused cultural misunderstandings not only with foreigners, but even with local subcultures such as the Navajo and those of Mexican and African descent. While the U.S. person of Northern European descent may be irritated by a Mexican arriving at 9 or 10 o'clock for an 8 o'clock party, the Mexican is dismayed over an invitation to a party which states in advance when it will be over. To the Mexican, this may indicate that such people do not know how to enjoy themselves.[4] Some authors have observed that the Japanese often find the U.S. people too time-bound, driven by schedules and deadlines. This has thwarted an easy development of relationships between the two groups of business people.[5]

There are advantages and disadvantages in both systems. While those who calculate time to the second and follow tight schedules may accomplish many tasks, they miss out on deep social relationships. The loneliness and pressure created by a strict time observation may lead to health problems such as high blood pressure, depression, general fatigue, eating disorders and some forms of cancer. Those with loose schedules accomplish less tasks but may experience a greater sense of security, deep personal relationships, less loneliness and less incidents of diseases such as high blood pressure and depression.

Norms can be defined as rules that guide behavior. While some norms are proscriptive, stating what must not be done, others are prescriptive, stressing what must be done. As Haviland[6] points out, standards that define what is "normal" are determined by the culture itself. The Aymara of the Bolivian Andes, for example, prohibit suicide, except in cases where an individual may be possessed by spirits of the dead, which cannot be exorcised. Given this type of affliction, suicide is considered to be a reasonable alternative.[7] It is important to note that culturally-induced conflicts not only can produce psychosis but can determine the type of psychosis as well. In a culture that encourages aggressiveness and suspicion, the crazy person is the one who is passive and trusting.[8]

Beliefs which directly or indirectly dictate what is right or wrong also differ from one culture to another. While the Higgi of Nigeria[9] believe that receiving anything with a left hand is a sign of bad manners, among the U.S. people, one needs to carefully monitor the use of particular fingers lest they should offend anyone. While non-Christian Japanese celebrate Christmas because the occasion sounds exciting and gets people off work, for the Christians, the occasion symbolizes spiritual renewal to welcome a savior. While the U.S. people believe in freedom of the press, speech, and association, these very qualities are regarded as highly dangerous and divisive among the Chinese who value kin ties and cooperation above everything else. For the Chinese, mutual dependence is the essence of all personal relationships, whereby compliance and subordination of one's will to that of the family and kin are of paramount importance.[10]

Beliefs are at the core of forming particular world views. The "rugged individualism" concept that is prevalent in the U.S. may not be well-regarded in Mexico even though they believe in "individuality." The U.S. people regard the individual as the center of attention, with ability to achieve anything through hard work. Anything that would get in the way of the individual's freedom to think, judge, and make decisions about how to live his or her life is not only morally wrong, but sacrilegious.[11] Mexicans, on the other hand, believe in the uniqueness of each individual, not so much as evident through actions and achievements, but through a person's inner qualities or soul (alma or espiritu). While the U.S. people might feel uncomfortable about using a word such as "soul" to describe an individual because it is regarded as too personal, the Mexicans might interpret the U.S. emphasis on objective words and rationality as a display of insensitive behavior. The Mexican interpretation is based on their belief in an emotional world, involving power and love-hate relationships.[12]

Emotions provide channels for self-expression. When and how to show emotion is very much regulated by culture. In the majority of cultures around the world, females are less restrained from showing emotion than males. However, even with such a generalization, cultures differ tremendously in how emotion is expressed. While it is not uncommon to meet young people on a U.S. college campus kissing and passionately involved with each other in a romantic fashion, such behavior is scorned or even considered taboo by Japanese, Africans, and Arabs. Even holding hands with someone of the opposite sex in public is considered impolite. Parents of such young people would be blamed for raising them without proper instructions.

Culture can also be expressed in terms of *attitudes* that people have toward life in general or some aspects of it. A futuristic attitude which is so typical of U.S. people is not common in other societies. One often hears a statement like, "See you tomorrow," while other people would say, "See you tomorrow, if God wishes." The former case shows a group of people who seem to have a handle on life and can almost predict with certainty that tomorrow will be here. In the latter case, events are usually left in the domain of a superior power, God. These kinds of attitudes definitely impact people's actions.

Aspirations which affect the goals that we design for ourselves and our perceptions of the world around us are related to attitudes. If a culture stresses friendship and cooperation, a stranger will be taken care of with great kindness and hospitality. On the other hand, if the culture emphasizes competition and individualism, a stranger will be looked upon with suspicion and sometimes open hostility and aggression.

Laws are also a major component of culture. What might be taken as social custom in one culture, may be law in another. Whereas a marriage license in the United States legalizes a marriage, in traditional Africa, parental consent is enough to make a marriage bond legal. Even in modern times where a license is necessary, a marriage without approval by the elders is not well regarded. Although a license may have been granted, there is always a fear that failure to be blessed by the wise, old people will render such a relationship weak from the start.

Finally, culture can be defined in terms of *symbols* that a group of people are associated with. A flag with fifty stars, white, blue and red colors and an eagle symbolizes the United States of America and so do very big cars. Movies that are shown abroad tend to portray the United States as a country with many rich people and plenty of guns. As these examples illustrate, some of our perceptions of a certain culture may be quite true and others may not be so true because they are based on a small sample of the population. I have seen many movies, for example, on Africa and almost in every case, there is an animal around. If it is not a lion, it is an elephant or a giraffe. The truth is that these animals are not so rampant or at least they don't roam about people's compounds as often as the movies tend to suggest. Just as perceiving the U.S. people in terms of abounding riches may to a large extent be a false image, the same is true of other cultures, too.

Each group of people tends to have its own self-definition which may or may not agree with outsiders' definitions.

Exercises

1. Find ten adjectives to describe your culture.
2. List everything you can think of that makes your culture distinct from the rest of the world.

FUNCTIONS OF CULTURE

Culture plays such significant roles in society that it may be perceived as the springboard of human activity. On a basic level, culture facilitates the *production* and *distribution* of goods and services that are necessary for survival. It is no wonder that so many modes of production are in operation all over the world. While some cultivate with hoes, others use plows and tractors. Besides dictating what tools to use in production, culture provides guidelines for the division of labor among people. Among the Batooro of Western Uganda, for example, it is the duty of men to work on the roof, while the Bagisu from the Eastern region of the same country expect the women to do this kind of work. The Masai of Western Kenya, on the other hand, expect the women to build the entire house. Table 2.1 illustrates how work is divided differently among various world cultures.

Systems of *education* can also reflect cultural differences. Whereas in many industrial societies, the role of education is played almost entirely by schools and other formal institutions of higher learning, this is not necessarily true in other parts of the world. The role of educating children to become responsible adults is played primarily by parents and to a lesser degree by schools. In such societies, children belong to the community and it is the responsibility of all older people around them to teach them proper ways of behaving. Usually the older people, who are considered to be wiser than younger ones due to their experience from many years of living are selected to be primary educators in society.

Besides education, culture also influences the way people think, thus influencing cross-cultural encounters. Most North Americans employ the *deductive* method of reasoning in order to solve problems. A person from such a cultural background may run into problems while interacting with a Korean who uses the *inductive* method. While the former is moving from broad categories to specific examples that rely on facts, the latter begins with specific observations and intuitive discovery in order to arrive at generalizations. Contrasting the western rational model of problem solving with the oriental intuitive approach, Culick notes the following:

> *The one develops and disciplines man's emotional nature, his sense of propriety, his aesthetic tastes; the other develops and disciplines the reason and will, the capacity to think and act independently. The one begets a culture of courtesy, the other a culture of realism.*[13]

TABLE 2.1 **The Division of Labor by Sex by 224 Societies**

Activity	Men Always	Men Usually	Either Sex	Women Usually	Women Always
Hunting	166	13	0	0	0
Trapping small animals	128	13	4	1	2
Herding	38	8	4	0	5
Fishing	98	34	19	3	4
Clearing agricultural land	73	22	17	5	13
Dairy operations	17	4	3	1	13
Preparing and planting soil	31	23	33	20	37
Erecting and dismantling shelter	14	2	5	6	22
Tending and harvesting crops	10	15	35	39	44
Bearing burdens	12	6	35	20	57
Cooking	5	1	9	28	158
Metalworking	78	0	0	0	0
Boat building	91	4	4	0	1
Working in stone	68	3	2	0	2
Basket making	25	3	10	6	82
Weaving	19	2	2	6	67
Manufacturing	12	3	8	9	95

Source: George P. Murdock, 1935.

Cultural differences can be reflected in the different learning styles that people from various cultural backgrounds exhibit. Bennett[14] observes that since U.S. schools tend to be monoethnic, this partly explains the high school dropout rates among Hispanics, Native Americans, and African Americans. Native-American students, for example, tend to approach tasks visually, preferring careful observation before performance, while learning their natural settings experientially. This is rooted in their culture which teaches basic skills such as hunting, tanning, and beadwork in a three-step sequence. As the adult teaches the young learner such tasks, the use of speech is minimal. When children from such an environment go to school and find themselves in a situation where emphasis is placed on verbal performance, culture shock sets in. If educators do not pay attention to these particular students' special needs, the results can be devastating. One common reaction is for such students to resort to silence, which might be interpreted as intellectual inferiority of learning disability.

A growing body of research shows that African-American children and youth who have been raised outside of the macroculture have a learning style that tends to be more relational as opposed to the analytical style typical of the mainstream culture. Their creativity in music, dance, religion, and dressing closely resembles that of their ancestors in Africa, even after centuries of living apart. This example illustrates the power of culture in molding behavior. It permeates patterns of thought and action and endures through generations. Hillard,[15] a prominent authority on race issues, notes that African Americans tend to respond to things in whole as opposed to their Euro-American counterparts who believe that anything can be subdivided into small parts. They tend to approximate space, numbers, and time instead of sticking to accuracy, and prefer inferential to deductive or inductive reasoning. Their tendency to focus on people rather than things partly explains why many of them go into helping professions such as psychology, teaching and social work. They are quick to perceive injustice and as a result tend to be altruistic. They tend to prefer novelty, freedom, and personal distinctiveness. They are also less word-dependent and very proficient in nonverbal communication.

Culture also serves to *maintain order* among members of a particular group. This may be done through formal means such as police, prisons, and the law. These kinds of institutions are particularly prevalent in industrial societies with complex technologies. Work is usually characterized by impersonal relationships, standardized codes of conduct, and well-spelled-out rules. In societies with simple technologies, characterized by strong family and community ties, order is maintained primarily by informal means. Cases that go to the police and courts are usually serious ones such as murder or robbery. Simple quarrels between neighbors and family members are usually dealt with by local community leaders. The particular culture sets guidelines to be followed in selecting community leaders. Seniority in age, a stable family structure, religious commitment, and good reputation are some of the very strong criteria for occupying a leadership position. While some cultures prefer males to be leaders, others select females.

It is also usually the role of a particular culture to design a system of *rewards* and *punishments* for a particular kind of behavior. While robbery may be punished by imprisonment in one culture, the robber will be stripped of his/her ears in another or might be whipped publicly in yet another culture. It is interesting to note that while U.S. parents punish their children by "grounding" them, thereby keeping them at home, in many other cultures, children are punished by sending them out of the house.

Another function of culture is to ensure that there is *biological continuity* through reproduction. The particular culture defines who should marry whom, when, and how. In cultures where there are royal clans, marriages are confined between people of particular clans for the sake of preserving the "royal blood" and keeping it from being diluted. Culture also dictates the number of children to be born. In Western cultures, fewer children are desired over many, while for Africans the larger the number of children, the better. As well as conferring status on the family, children are often regarded as a source of economic strength and insurance in old age. It is no wonder that several family planning programs have met with failure in cases where they have not been adapted to the local cultural expectations.

Finally, culture *motivates* its members to engage in activities for survival. Through various symbols, members of different cultures define the meaning of life and are either motivated or discouraged from engaging in certain activities. An example of motivating symbols is beauty standards which differ from culture to culture. While U.S. women strive to lose weight constantly, a beautiful African woman should not be excessively skinny. In fact, among the Baganda of Central Uganda and Banyankole of Western Uganda, large hips are a sign of beauty. To be excessively thin, especially for a woman, may indicate a bad marriage or poverty. It could also be a sign of an impending depression.

Exercise

List as many symbols (these could be objects or body gestures) as you can that are prevalent in your culture. Match each symbol with the image or object that it represents. Share your list with the class.

CHARACTERISTICS OF CULTURE

Culture has certain fundamental characteristics that distinguish it from other concepts. Its *integrative* nature shows all aspects of a culture to function as an interrelated whole. It is, for example, difficult to separate the role of education from that of governance, family, health, and economic activity. Although, for example, in the United States, the constitution spells out a separation between church and state, in many other countries, the religious institution is an arm of the government. In such systems, the head of state is the rightful head of the religious institution. The Queen of England, for example, is also the head of the Church of England.

Another characteristic of culture is that it is *shared* and *learned*, rather than being biologically determined. All cultures specify different guidelines for the same type of behavior. For example, it is all right for a U.S. person to carry food to meetings and eat while business is going on. It is terribly impolite for a Mutooro from Western Uganda to behave in this way. It is particularly rude if the person who is eating is an authority figure, such as a professor in front of students. The same principle operates regarding clothes. People learn through socialization that certain attire is all right for some occasions and not others. While a U.S. professor, business leader, or politician can wear shorts to the office on a hot day, this behavior is associated with lack of dignity in many other societies, namely the Middle East, Asia, and Africa. Whereas the U.S. people value informality, this same trait may be associated with insecurity, poor education, low self-esteem, and lack of money in Japan and many other societies. In those societies, being "dressed up" is the right thing to do, especially for an authority figure demanding respect.

Another example of how different cultures teach their members differently regards time. I remember when I was growing up being told that I should stop hurrying and behave like a "lady." People of dignity are not expected to run around. It is assumed that time will always be around; therefore, in order to command respect, one had better slow down. Children and those with less power can run around; after all, they have nothing to lose. Older and powerful people have a lot to lose in terms of respect if they are always "chasing after time." This may sound very surprising to a person brought up in a society where time is cherished as a rare commodity that should be guarded jealously. In these societies, excessive slowness could be interpreted to mean laziness or poor health.

When one violates norms of a particular culture, he/she may be rejected and isolated from the rest of the group. My mother told me recently that all my relatives know me very well. After probing, she told me that they know me as a strict time-keeper. She added that they often wonder what I am like now since I live in a culture that is always chasing after time. I assured her that I had no problem with that and she replied, "I know."

CULTURE ACQUISITION

The process of learning cultural expectations is a gradual one. Through socialization, which begins at birth and ends at death, people learn cultural scripts from societies of which they are a part. During this process, people learn, through interaction with others, what they must know in order to survive and function within their society. The poem below illustrates the power of words in the socialization process.

Learn Our Way

Please my child
Yes, dear child
Learn our way
This is to say
Follow our way
And never stray
Stand by us
And do not fuss
You'll find a reward
To move forward.

(Kabagarama, 1993)

Learning cultural scripts can be an easy process or a hard one, depending on what is being learned. Learning to sit at the table or on the floor during meals sounds easy enough, but training to be a good warrior is not so easy. The rite of passage marking a child's change from youth to adulthood can be fairly simple or complicated by rituals such as those involving circumcision. Using words in speech can be a fairly simple process, once the person learns how to speak, but the process gets complicated when individuals have to speak certain words to some categories of people and not others. Simple words like "Sir," "Madam," "Girl," "Boy," "Man," and "Woman" often carry different meanings when used in different contexts. Bornlund[16] states that differences in meaning rather than vocabulary isolate cultures and cause them to regard each other as strange or even barbaric. He adds that it is not too surprising that many cultures refer to themselves as "The People," relegating all other human beings to a subhuman form of life.

Exercise

List commandments (do's and don'ts) that were given to you as you were growing up.

AGENTS OF CULTURE

Culture is transmitted from one generation to another through various channels. In technologically advanced societies where almost every home has a *television* set, this becomes a significant learning medium. Messages that are usually sent out to women regarding "ideal" body sizes, hair styles, and features can be used as illustrations. If, for example, an ideal beautiful woman is portrayed as thin, blond, and blue-eyed, what happens to those who do not fit this ideal model? Unless they are told of different beauty standards by other sources, television images can cause these women a lot of frustration. This frustration can either be simple and ignorable or it can be extreme, resulting in serious psychological problems such as eating disorders.

Traditionally, people learned their cultural scripts from *families, peers, schools, religious groups, work organizations* and all other groups they associated with. Of all these agents, the family is the most powerful, since its role begins when the child is born. To ensure that children learn what is expected of them, families have systems of rewards for those who learn well and punishments for those who deviate. Punishments could range from a disapproving glance to a spanking, public ridicule, or withdrawal of certain rights such as inheritance.

In technologically advanced societies, schools and peers play a very significant role in the socialization process. For someone who has not grown up in such a setting, it is surprising to see how influential teenagers can be on each other. In many non-Western societies, teenagers tend to identify more with their parents and to a lesser extent with peers. Boys are expected to help their fathers in tasks such as building homes and looking after domestic animals. Girls are expected to help mothers in cooking, taking care of the children and looking after the fields. It is almost unheard of to find parents paying their own children to look after their siblings. If any reward is given, it is indirect in the form of extra clothes, praise, or pocket money, but not calculated hourly wages.

Besides the family, peers, and television, religious organizations have a strong influence on shaping people's behavior. A Catholic who has been socialized to make the sign of the cross may at times wonder if those who are not making the sign are serious about their prayers. On the other hand, a Protestant raised differently will not appreciate such an act and may tend to explain it away as mere ritualism.

Finally, work organizations, especially in technologically complex societies, play a major role in shaping people's behavior. No wonder many people find life very boring and at times unbearable upon retirement. They have, over the years, been used to such routine activities as going to the office at a certain time, eating lunch at a certain time, and going home at a certain time that a change in this schedule upsets their whole life system.

Work organizations in different cultures have similarities and differences in socializing their employees. Regardless of the society in question, employees usually report to work and leave at a particular time. There are common uniforms that characterize certain professions. A doctor, for example, usually wears a white coat. However, other codes of conduct depend on the culture in question. In Japan, for example, loyalty, teamwork and "proper" manners are expected at work. It is not uncommon to see people bow when talking to their superiors. In the United States the emphasis placed on individualism, success, competition, and freedom sometimes undermines teamwork and loyalty.

Examples cited in this chapter show that culture is a strong influence on human behavior. Bornlund[17] clearly states that cultural norms surround people and permeate thought and action. This process is so thorough that few ever recognize the assumptions on which their lives and sanity rest. Because they occupy a symbolic universe governed by codes that are unconsciously acquired and automatically employed, they may not notice that the ways in which they interpret and talk about events are different from the ways people from other cultures conduct their affairs.

It is, therefore, very important that people from different cultural backgrounds get along with each other and learn from one another. Such contact not only broadens their experiences, but is necessary in a world ravaged by conflict and war. It is a gateway to creating a more peaceful world to live in. Both from a humanitarian and political/economic standpoint, knowledge of other cultures and respect for those who are different are plausible ventures.

DISCUSSION TOPICS

1. To what extent does cultural misunderstanding contribute to national and international conflict?
2. How has the cultural setting in which you were brought up influenced your outlook on life?

EXERCISES

1. Divide into small groups of five people and list the following:
   a. Favorite food of each group member
   b. Favorite music of each member
   c. Clothes that each member likes to wear and for what occasion(s).
2. Share the information obtained from small group discussions of exercise number one with the large group. Pay attention to similarities and differences.
3. Each participant should try and answer the question: "Why do I like the food, music, and clothes that I suggested in exercise number one?" After a few minutes of quiet thinking, members should share their responses.
4. Complete the following sentences individually:

   a. My culture is _____

   b. I like my culture because _____

   c. I began learning about my culture _____

   d. I will stop learning about my culture _____

   e. I learn about my culture from _____

   f. If I had a chance to change one aspect of my culture, I would change _____

5. List all cultures and subcultures to which you belong. (Cultures constitute large entities such as the Chinese or U.S. cultures, while subcultures refer to small groupings within the large ones. Examples of subcultures include Catholic, Mexican-American, etc.)
   a. Rank those cultures and subcultures in order of importance to you.
   b. List the advantages and disadvantages of belonging to the cultures and subcultures that you have identified.

6. Imagine yourself a teacher in an elementary school. A new student whose parents have just moved into your town from a foreign country joins your class.
   a. Outline steps that you are going to take in order to make this student comfortable.
   b. How are you going to prepare your class, which is culturally homogeneous to accept this new student?
7. As a group, design a method to test intelligence that is as culturally unbiased as possible.

ENDNOTES

1. Michael C. Howard, *Contemporary Cultural Anthropology* (Glenview: Scott, Foresman and Company, 1989).
2. William A. Haviland, *Cultural Anthropology* (New York: Holt, Rinehart and Winston, Inc., 1987).
3. R. Bellah, R. Madsen, W. Sullivan, A. Swindler and S. Tipton, *Habits of the Heart: Individualism and Commitment in American Life* (New York: Harper & Row, 1985).
4. John Condon, "So Near the United States: Notes on Communication Between Mexicans and North Americans," *Intercultural Communication: A Reader*, eds. Larry A. Samovar and Richard E. Porter (Belmont: Wadsworth Publishing Company, 1991), 106-112.
5. Ibid.
6. William A. Haviland, ibid.
7. Ibid., 133.
8. Ibid., 134.
9. Samuel Dali, Personal Interview (McPherson College, 1991).
10. Francis L.K. Hsu, "The Cultural Problem of the Cultural Anthropologist," *American Anthropologist 81* (1979), 58.
11. R. Bellah, et al., ibid.: vii, 142.
12. John Condon, ibid.
13. S. Culick, *The East and West: A Study of Their Psychic and Cultural Characteristics* (Ruthland: Charles Turtle, 1962), 68.
14. Christine I. Bennett, *Comprehensive Multicultural Education* (Boston: Allyn and Bacon, 1990).
15. A. Hillard, "Alternatives to IQ Testing: An Approach to the Identification of Gifted Minority Children" (Final Report to the California State Department of Education, 1976).
16. Dean c. Bornlund, *Communicative Styles of Japanese and Americans: Images and Realities.* (Belmont: Wadsworth Publishing Co., 1989).
17. Ibid.

▶ 3

Communication: The Heartbeat of Human Interaction

Miller and Steinberg have defined *communication* as a process whereby one person deliberately attempts to convey meaning to another.[1] They imply that we communicate with the intention of attempting to modify behavior. Words are selected and organized in such a way as to have maximum impact on the individual whose behavior we are trying to modify.

However, Ruesch and Bateson[2] have argued that communication is not always aimed at modifying behavior. They stress the unintended messages that very often get communicated and greatly impact behavior. Scholars of this view define communication as a process that takes place whenever meaning is attached to messages. This can take place even when the sender did not intend the message to be part of the process. A group of people could be at a long meeting, for example, where one of the members yawns unintentionally. This very act may be interpreted as a signal to end the meeting. It could also suggest that the group leader is boring or that the person who is yawning did not have enough sleep the previous night.

Samovar and Porter[3] suggest that communication occurs whenever meaning is attributed to behavior or its residue. On entering an elevator, for example, someone may smell the perfume of a person who previously rode on this same elevator. A conclusion could be reached that the person who wore the perfume is very rich. On the other hand, another conclusion might be that the person who wore the perfume is going on a date. When such conclusions are made, communication has taken place. Residue takes into account consequences of past experiences, which are very often culture-related.

Whatever approach is used to define communication, it is important to note that this process is critical to human existence. It is through communication that human beings have accomplished tasks such as lighting fire or going to the moon. It is important to recognize that people from different cultures communicate differently. In recognizing this fact, we come to understand each other better as we patiently listen to one another.

Hall,[4] in an attempt to provide a theoretical framework for understanding cross-cultural communication, classifies world cultures into two categories: *low* and *high context*. Although simple and sometimes limited in generalizability, the model offers a starting point into the study of this intricate subject.

According to Hall, in low-context cultures, examples of which include the United States and northern Europe, meaning is derived from the message itself, which might be in the form of a spoken word, a memo, or a computer program. Among high-context cultures, such as East Asian, Arab, Southern European, Native American, and Latin American, meanings are derived from the context in which the communication takes place. To this list can be added the Africans, the majority of whom share the proverb, "Ebiikara munda bisemeza amalembo" which means words which are left unsaid leave the paths clean. Bennett summarizes Hall's scheme in Table 3.1.[5]

There are remarkable differences between communication patterns of people from low- and high-context cultures. Stewart[6] notes, for example, that because U.S. people emphasize rationality, they assume that events can be explained and reasons for their occurrence determined. They see the world as composed of facts from which ideas can be generated, thus the emphasis on explicit meaning. Arabs and Asians, on the other hand, look for the implicit level and metaphoric association in messages. In Arab culture, poetry, plays, and story-telling are regarded as inspired language because they portray an image of a well-educated speaker, capable of rendering judgment and advice. There is a high value placed on the persuasive power, rhythm, and sound of words because these heighten the impact of the message.[7] This is unlike the dominant U.S. style of speech in which communication is individualistic, whereby each communicator is a separate individual, engaging in diverse communicative activities to maximize self-interest, usually by persuasion.[8]

Differences in communication patterns can be noted even among the various subcultures in the United States. As Kochman[9] points out, for example, African-American speech patterns have been ignored for a long time based on the assumption that they need to operate according to speech patterns established by the dominant Caucasians. During the mid-1960s, schools were committed to eradicating the African-American language patterns for they were regarded as "improper." More recently, educators have begun to sense that the African-American language is functional, particularly when the people are communicating with those from their communities.

According to Kochman, African-American and Caucasian speech patterns are different. On observing a meeting between African-American community leaders and faculty representatives in Chicago, he observed that the two groups hardly understood one another's speech patterns. While the faculty thought the behavior of the community leaders did not meet requirements for rational discussion and called it a "Baptist revival meeting" or "pep rally," the faculty were considered lacking in sincerity, honest conviction and sometimes "devious."[10]

Debates between students from the two cultural backgrounds produced similar results. The African-American speech patterns were high-keyed, animated, interpersonal, confrontational, and affect-generating. The Caucasians were low-keyed, dispassionate, impersonal, nonchallenging and without affect. The author suggests that because the two groups have different perceptions about certain aspects of reality, their speech patterns are bound to differ. The African-Americans often use argument as a way to test their own

TABLE 3.1 **Summary of Hall's Conception of Culture According to Context**

	High Context	Low Context
Time	*Polychronic* Loose schedules, flux, multiple simultaneous activities. Last minute changes of important plans. Time is less tangible.	*Monochronic* Tight schedules, one event at a time, linear. Importance of being on time. Time is more tangible (e.g., is spent, wasted, is "money").
Space & Tempo	*High-Sync* Synchrony, moving in harmony with others and with nature, is consciously valued. Social rhythm has meaning.	*Low-Sync* Synchrony is less noticeable. Social rhythm is underdeveloped.
Reasoning	*Comprehensive Logic* Knowledge is gained through intuition, spiral logic, and contemplation. Importance of feelings.	*Linear Logic* Knowledge is gained through analytical reasoning (e.g., the Socratic method). Importance of words.
Verbal Messages	*Restricted Codes* "Shorthand speech," reliance on nonverbal and contextual cues. Overall emotional quality more important than meaning of particular words. Economical, fast, efficient communication that is satisfying; slow to change; fosters interpersonal cohesiveness and provides for human need for social stability. Stress on social integration and harmony; being polite.	*Elaborate Codes* Verbal amplification through extended talk or writing. Little reliance on nonverbal or contextual cues. Doesn't foster cohesiveness but can change rapidly. Provides for human need to adapt and change. Stress on argument and persuasion; being direct.

Source: Christine I. Bennett, 1990; pp. 55-56.

views. This is deeply rooted in their oral tradition whereby a scholar acts as an advocate for the material presented. Struggle for a particular position is viewed positively because it shows that one very much cares about the idea. There is also an assumption that ideas become authoritative by being tested through argument. In debates, therefore, reference is constantly made to the initiator of the idea and there is concern for the argument as well as the art through which it is expressed; thus the use of body language. Caucasians, on the other hand, equate confrontation with conflict and try to avoid it as much as possible. Because this culture separates the material from the presenter, how a person feels about

TABLE 3.1 *continued*

	High Context	**Low Context**
Social Roles	*Tight Social Structure* Individual's behavior is predictable; conformity to role expectations.	*Loose Social Structure* Behavior is unpredictable; role behavior expectations are less clear.
Interpersonal Relations	*Group Is Paramount* Clear status distinctions (e.g., age, rank, position), strong distinctions between insiders and outsiders. Human interactions are emotionally based, person oriented. Stronger personal bonds, bending of individual interests for sake of relationships. Cohesive, highly interrelated human relationships, completed action chains. Members of group are first and foremost.	*Individual Is Paramount* Status is more subtle, distinctions between insiders and outsiders less important. Human interactions are functionally based, approach is specialized. Fragile, interpersonal bonds due to geographic mobility. Fragmented, short-term human relationships, broken action chains when relationship is not satisfying. Individuals are first, groups come second.
Social Organization	*Personalized Law and Authority* Customary procedures and who one knows are important. Oral agreements are binding. In face of unresponsive bureaucracies, must be an insider or have a "friend" to make things happen (e.g., going through the "back door"). People in authority are personally and truly responsible for actions of every subordinate.	*Procedural Law and Authority* Procedures, laws and policies are more important than who one knows. Written contracts are binding. Policy rules, unresponsive bureaucracy. People in authority try to pass the buck. Impersonal Legal procedures

the idea is not fundamental to its value—"The truth of the matter is in the matter."[11] Ideas derive authority through publication or they are certified by experts in the field. This assumption limits the role of the presenter, often making such an individual appear overly impersonal. While African-Americans may view the Caucasian style as an avoidance of responsibility or evasive, their style may be viewed by the latter as "too emotional." To sum up the African-American communication style, Harrison[12] notes that there is usually a high spiritual intensity based on the assumption that internal forces are controlled by the structure and mode through which they are released—"An emotion is never out of control when it fits the modality it is released in."[13]

INGREDIENTS OF COMMUNICATION

A model presented by Shannon and Weaver[14] includes the following communication components: the *sender*, the *message*, and the *receiver* of the message. The sender engages in the process of *encoding*, that is, converting an idea into a set of symbols to be communicated. Such symbols are transmitted through a *medium*. The message is comprised of symbols which have to be *decoded* by the receiver. The decoding process involves an interpretation of the message's semantic content. In addition, Shannon and Weaver suggest that usually the message is interrupted by "noise."

They add that whatever is communicated is merely a sign that stands for some meaning that we read into it. The signs in the message have meaning that we give them as a result of our experiences. Distortions may occur if the sender's encoding and the receiver's decoding do not converge. This happens if their shared frame of reference is minimal, causing the message to mean different things to each.

Hopman[15] suggests that the greater the gap between the shared experiences of individual senders and receivers of messages, the greater the differences in their interpretations of the same messages and hence, the greater the distortion in the process of communication. He also stipulates that the greater the noise or random disturbance in a communication channel, the greater the distortion in the communication process. Individual traits and geocultural factors also play a big role in influencing communication. These are usually very difficult to interpret, particularly if the communicating parties come from different cultural backgrounds.

INDIVIDUAL TRAITS

When people communicate with one another, they bring to the situation their whole state of being, comprised of sentiments, values, emotions, attitudes, and physical dispositions. It is therefore important that we know as much as we can about the person we are interacting with in order to avoid a misinterpretation of the information received. Research has found age, race, and gender to be key variables in influencing communication across cultures. A number of studies have, for instance, observed differences between various categories of people in their use of space while communicating with one another. Dean[16] observed that adults tend to react more favorably to an invasion of their space by children than fellow adults. Curt and Nine's[17] research concluded that in Puerto Rico, people of the same age and gender touch more and stand closer to each other during conversation than those who differ in the two characteristics. When relationships between males and females are close, females do touch males but males rarely reciprocate. Shuter's[18] study, which included Costa Ricans, Colombians, and Panamanians, observed that directness of interactions diminishes as one travels from Central to South America. The mean distances between the communicating parties in Costa Rica were much smaller. The same study observed that more Costa Ricans touched each other than the others did. However, for all three, there was more contact between female/female dyads, followed by female/male, and lastly, male/male dyads.

A study of the differences in personal space needs among Hispanic, Caucasian, and African-Americans conducted by Baxter[19] arrived at interesting conclusions. Overall, mixed-race dyads exhibited greater distance than any single-race pair. Bauer,[20] in an attempt to assess use of personal space among African-Americans and Caucasians, observed significant differences between the two groups. When instructed to approach same race, same gender confederates to the highest level of comfort in personal space, Caucasian males stood farthest, followed by Caucasian females, then African-American males, and finally African-American females who stood closest. It is important to note that theories of contact versus noncontact hold in same-culture interactions, speaking the native language. Sussman and Rosenfeld[21] observed that Japanese, Venezuelan, and U.S. student dyads all maintained farther distances when speaking a foreign language. His conclusion was that both culture and language influence conversational distance.

GEOCULTURAL FACTORS

Geocultural factors include such things as the location where interaction is taking place, climate, time of the conversation, and the discussion topic. If, for example, one of the parties is from a cold climate and the other from a warm one, their conversation will be affected by these climatic differences. While someone from a cold climate may spend a great deal of time talking about the beautiful spring flowers, the one from the warm climate where flowers are seen all year round might find such conversation boring. The same may be true with regard to other types of nature. I remember an English girl with whom I shared a house while both of us taught at a high school in Western Uganda. The girl often talked about butterflies and asked me to accompany her to the woods to catch some. Although I found this conversation extremely boring, I decided to go with her out of courtesy. I had a very difficult time convincing my relatives that catching butterflies was a worthwhile exercise.

Time is important because it puts a certain routine in people's lives. In one culture, evenings may be times to be with one's family whereas in another, it is time to get out and be with friends. While supper time may be around six o'clock for one group of people, it may be nine o'clock for another. When people with different body clocks are interacting, they may not understand each other's behavior. I remember struggling with the idea that I had to eat dinner around six o'clock in the United States, whereas the same activity took place between eight and nine o'clock in the culture where I grew up.

Events such as birth, death, graduation from college, and marriage are interpreted differently by various cultures. While, for example, among the Igbo of Nigeria, the bride-to-be dances before the potential in-laws, this is not the case among traditional Batooro of Western Uganda. The young lady is expected to show sorrow because she is about to leave her family. In some cases, brides are pinched by their aunts in order to evoke tears or to at least show a sorrowful face. Although this no longer goes on among the more educated groups, it is still common among traditional families.

THE ROLE OF VERBAL COMMUNICATION

Sapir[22] observes that human beings do not live in the objective world alone. They are very much at the mercy of the particular language which has become the medium of expression for their society. It is through language that people conceptualize the world around them. Languages differ so much in grammar and structure that no two languages can be considered as representing the same social reality.

Hoijer,[23] in his study among the Navajo of Arizona and New Mexico, observed that their grammar emphasizes movement, specifying the nature, direction and status of such movement because they perceive the universe to be in motion. While the English speakers would say, "One dresses," "One is young," "He is carrying a round object," the Navajo counterpart would say, "One moves into clothing," "One moves about newly," "He moves along handling a round object." This motion is deeply rooted in Navajo mythology whereby the gods and culture heroes move restlessly from place to place, seeking to perfect the universe.[24]

Verbal communication plays a very significant role in human communication. All languages use a limited number of sounds to refer to many objects and experiences, thus making human language very efficient. Another quality that makes human language unique is its productivity. The same set of words can be used to convey different meanings, if arranged differently. The following example illustrates this point.

> *I went there to watch the only game.*
> *I went there only to watch the game.*
> *Only I went there to watch the game.*

The subject of death is handled differently depending on the culture in question. I remember one day when my husband came home from attending a funeral, the first one in the U.S. He said to me, "Dear, I am going to tell you this but it is very frightening." He continued to say that he did not witness the burial of the dead person. The coffin had been left on top of the ground. My remark was, "Oh my goodness; we are dead!" You can tell from both of our remarks that this was a major violation of our belief system. Where we were raised, the dead aren't considered buried until one throws soil in the grave. This process is known as "Kunagina akataka," in my Tooro language. As a matter of fact, that night we were so scared that we hardly fell asleep. Well, we have attended many more funerals in the U.S. and are getting used to the idea, gradually although we still feel that it is not "right."

Samovar and Porter[25] add that human language has the ability to communicate something or some idea that is not in the immediate environment. Things that took place in the past are described and so are those that are to happen in the future. In addition, the displacement nature of human language creates room for hypothetical thinking. The ability to think in abstract terms that is characteristic of human beings is influenced by culture. Important images like that of God are culture specific and so are expressions of various emotions such as anger, pain, joy, love, and sorrow.

NONVERBAL COMMUNICATION

Samovar and Porter[26] suggest that nonverbal communication has several uses. It helps us learn about the *affective* or *emotional* states of others. Someone saying "I am fine," with a frown is in a different emotional state from someone who says it with a smile. We also get first *impressions* of others from nonverbal communication. This type of communication also helps in *repeating* messages. After offering a seat to someone, for example, pointing to the actual chair confirms the offer and assures the receiver that the speaker is serious about it.

Nonverbal communication also *complements* verbal messages. Food offered with a smile, for example, is much better received. Messages can also be contradicted by nonverbal communication. Many African languages use parables and poetic forms of expression. Upon arrival at someone's residence for example, the host may say, "I am not greeting you. Where have you been all these months?" These words may sound frightening to someone who does not understand the culture. From the nonverbal expressions, this same person may be expressing joy and a lot of affection. Alternatively, the host may welcome the visitor by dancing or singing without necessarily saying any words of welcome.

Another use of nonverbal communication is *substituting* gestures for words. While members of a U.S. football team may make the "thumbs up" sign after a victory, this same gesture is a curse among the Batooro because the "master" finger is being pointed at someone. Nonverbal communication can also be used to *regulate* conversation. While at a meeting, one person could signal another to start speaking by a certain look. The same is true for a choir director who uses gestures as a way of telling the group to perform in a certain way.

In addition to the uses outlined by Samovar and Porter, nonverbal communication can also play the role of *correcting*, *shielding*, *excluding*, and *positioning*. There are times when we want to correct an error that was made during a certain conversation and may feel embarrassed or afraid to apologize in words. This mistake can be corrected by using nonverbal messages. Lovers who have just had a fight, for example, may embrace each other after a while as a sign of reconciliation. The person who started the fight may initiate the embrace as a sign of admitting to a mistake that was made. Reconciliatory behavior is interpreted differently by various cultures. While flowers may please a U.S. woman and convince her that her lover is sorry, the African woman may interpret this act as merely playing games. I witnessed an interesting experience. One couple that had just moved from an African country to the U.S. were having marital problems. They decided to consult with their Caucasian church leader. Among other suggestions, the pastor advised the husband to take flowers to his wife and apologize for his mistakes. Well, do you want to guess where the flowers ended up? If you guessed the trash can, you are wrong. They ended up in his face. Don't get me wrong; Africans like flowers. However, they were used out of context. While they might be used to decorate a house, they may not be successful at resolving a major conflict between a husband and wife. Although they look beautiful, flowers in Africa grow all year round and some of them grow wild. Their value, while compared to an item such as jewelry, cloth, a goat or a cow is very low.

Languages have taboo words that are not spoken very often or are excluded from certain company. In such cases, nonverbal communication protects people from saying words that might be embarrassing. Instead of saying "shut up" or "keep quiet" to someone, a certain look or "shh" said softly prevents ill feelings that could result from harsh words.

When people do not want to include others in their conversation, they usually do not tell them directly, especially if they are adults. By observing the nonverbal communication, the person who is not wanted as part of the conversation knows and can leave. While in some cultures the exclusion is done primarily by manipulating space and altering body posture, other groups may stop conversation or the intruders may be looked at in such a way as to suggest that this conversation is not meant for them.

In every culture, status is conferred on people in different ways. From nonverbal cues, we can rank ourselves in society. This view agrees with Charles Horton Cooley's[27] idea of the "looking-glass self." He suggests that our image is a function of what other members of society confer on us. Concepts such as "beauty," "charm," "power," and "failure" are in and of themselves meaningless until other members of society use them either directly or indirectly in reference to us.

THE ROLE OF SILENCE IN COMMUNICATION

A great deal can be learned about a culture from the way it treats silence. Bruneau[28] points out that silences are not only based in the very comprehensibility of each world language but they are also the stuff out of which social acts, social actions, social presence, and social events are created and articulated. Customs, traditions, social mannerisms, social stability, and normative actions can all be viewed as they relate to habitual silences. There is an interdependent relationship between speech and silence.

The role of silence in the communication process is interpreted differently in every culture. Whereas the Western tradition views silence and ambiguity negatively, in Far Eastern cultures there is a bias toward silence. Bruneau[29] observes that there is a general misconception in the West regarding silence. The U.S. culture, for example, interprets it to mean sorrow, critique, obligation, regret, or embarrassment. The Japanese, on the other hand, have a mistrust for verbal skills, thinking that these tend to show superficiality in contrast to inner, less articulate innuendo.[30] In this culture, anticipatory communication is common, whereby the listener has to guess and accommodate the speaker's needs. Sensitivity and "catching on" quickly to the unsaid meaning are very valuable skills, showing intelligence[31]

AN ASSESSMENT

This chapter has highlighted the importance of communication in human interaction. While different languages use specific words to convey certain meanings, many messages are transmitted nonverbally. It is therefore not enough to learn other languages in order to understand how other people live. It is equally necessary to place particular words in their proper contexts and to recognize the importance of nonverbal cues in fostering human understanding.

DISCUSSION TOPICS

1. Show ways in which your first language has influenced your outlook on life.
2. With other members of your group, discuss various ways in which your language takes people from other cultures for granted.
3. How is learning a foreign language beneficial to an individual?
4. What sounds can't you make because you are limited by your first language?
5. With examples, discuss various ways in which nonverbal communication is used to convey messages in your culture.

EXERCISES

1. Write ten words in your native language.
   a. List as many alternative ways of saying the same ten words as you can think of (using the same language).
   b. Look up the same ten words in at least two other languages.
2. Look for someone from another country who lives in your community. Interview that person with regard to what shocked him/her about your culture. Write a summary of your findings from the interview and share these with your group or class. Pay particular attention to differences brought about by language.
3. Visit a popular shopping place on a busy day and observe the people for one or two hours.
   a. Make note of how people communicate both verbally and nonverbally.
   b. Write a brief report of your experience, paying particular attention to the similarities and differences between the behavior of the people you observed and your own.
   c. Divide into two groups of equal sizes. Each group member should use a nonverbal cue. Members of the same group should try to guess what the cue stands for. Each correct guess is worth a point. After three attempts without success, the other group is given a chance and if they guess it, they get the point. The game ends when either group scores up to 20 points, after which another round can begin.
4. List as many taboo words in your language as possible. Why are these words considered taboo?

ENDNOTES

1. Gerald R. Miller and Mark Steinberg, *Between People: A New Analysis of Interpersonal Communication* (Chicago: Science Research Associates, 1975).
2. Jurgen Reusch, "Values, Communication, and Culture," *Communication: The Social Matrix of Psychiatry*, ed. Jurgen Ruesch and Gregory Bateson (New York: W. W. Norton, 1951), 5–6.
3. Lary A. Samovar and Richard E. Porter, *Intercultural Communication: A Reader* (Belmont: Wadsworth Publishing Company, 1991), 28.
4. E. T. Hall, *The Hidden Dimension* (New York: Doubleday, 1966); *Beyond Culture* (New York: Doubleday, 1976).

5. Christine I. Bennett, *Comprehensive Multicultural Education* (Boston: Allyn and Bacon, 1990), 55–56.
6. Edward Stewart, *American Cultural Patterns: A Cross-Cultural Perspective* (Yarmouth: Intercultural Press, 1985).
7. Samuel H. Hammod, "Arab and Moslem Rhetorical Theory," *Central States Speech Journal* (1963), 97–102.
8. R. Bellah, R. Madsen, W. Sullivan, A. Swindler and S. Tipton, *Habits of the Heart: Individualism and Commitment in American Life* (New York: Harper & Row, 1985).
9. Thomas Kochman, *Black and White Styles in Conflict* (Chicago: The University of Chicago Press, 1981).
10. Ibid., 14.
11. Ibid., 21.
12. Paul C. Harrison, *The Drama of Nommo* (New York: Grove, 1972), xv.
13. Ibid., 157.
14. Claude E. Shannon and Warren Weaver, *The Mathematical Theory of Communication* (Urbana: University of Illinois Press, 1949).
15. Terrence P. Hopmann, "Communication and Bargaining in International Diplomacy," *Intercultural and International Communication*, ed. Fred Casmir (Washington, D.C.: University of American Press, 1978), 579–613.
16. L. M. Dean, F. N. Willis and J. N. LaRocco, "Invasion of Personal Space as a Function of Age, Sex and Race" (*Psychological Reports*, 1976), 959–965.
17. C. Curt and J. Nine, "Hispanic-Anglo Conflicts in Non-Verbal Communication," *Perspectives Pedagogicas*, ed. Isidora Albina (San Juan, Puerto Rico: Universidad de Puerto Rico, 1983).
18. Robert Shuter, "Non-Verbal Communication: Proxemics and Tactility in Latin America," *Journal of Communication 26* (1976), 46–52.
19. J. Baxter, "Interpersonal Spacing in Natural Settings," *Sociometry 33* (1970), 444–456.
20. E. A. Bauer "Personal Space: A Study of Blacks and Whites," *Sociometry 36* (1973), 402–408.
21. N. Sussman and H. M. Rosenfeld, "Influence of Culture, Language and Sex on Conversation distance," *Journal of Personality and Social Psychology 42* (1982), 66–74.
22. Edward Sapir, "The Status of Linguistics as a Science," *The Selected Writings of Edward Sapir in Language, Culture and Personality*, ed. David Mandelbaum (Berkeley: University of California Press, 1949), 160–166.
23 Harry Hoijer, "Cultural Implications of Some Navajo Linguistic Categories," *Language in Culture and Society*, ed. D. Hymes (New York: Harper & Row), 142–160.
24. Ibid.
25. Larry A. Samovar and Richard E. Porter (ibid.), 180–182.
26. Ibid.
27. Charles H. Cooley, *Human Nature and the Social Order* (New York: Scribner's, 1902–1904).
28. T. J. Bruneau, "Communicative Silences: Forms and Functions," *Journal of Communication 56* (1973), 17–46.
29. Ibid.

30. E. Reischauer, *The Japanese* (Cambridge, Mass.: Harvard University Press, 1977).
31. T. S. Lebra, *Japanese Patterns of Behavior* (Honolulu: The University Press of Hawaii, 1976).

► 4

The Seven-Step Process (T.S.S.P.) of Cross-Cultural Understanding

Dealing with people whose cultures are different from ours can be very pleasant or very painful. It is painful when we do not adequately prepare ourselves for the experience, thereby making ourselves prone to misconceptions and confusion. A process has been developed through which we can learn basic rules about understanding people of other cultures. The seven-step model, presented in Figure 4.1 moves us from the start of the encounter, to the getting acquainted stage, and to the final stage of establishing trust and cooperation. The inner, dotted circle shows that the process of cross-cultural understanding is not simple or clear cut. Very often, we have to go back and forth between the different stages and at times we need to start the whole process over again. The four letters stand for "The Seven-Step Process."

GETTING ACQUAINTED

When we encounter people whose cultures are different from ours, we experience uncertainty. Although we may genuinely want to get close to them, we fear rejection. A common reaction at the beginning of the encounter is, "How do I handle this?" This honest question is only the beginning. Instead of opting to "give someone space," start getting acquainted. When in doubt, remember that those very people you are worried about may also be uncertain and fearful.

In many cultures around the world, the host is expected to make the first move. Newcomers expect to be made as comfortable as possible, especially if they have been invited. In fact, visitors are treated so well that the host family will go out of its way to provide special food and sleeping arrangements. The hosts do not want to make a bad impression on visitors, since such people are their "ambassadors" to other cultures.

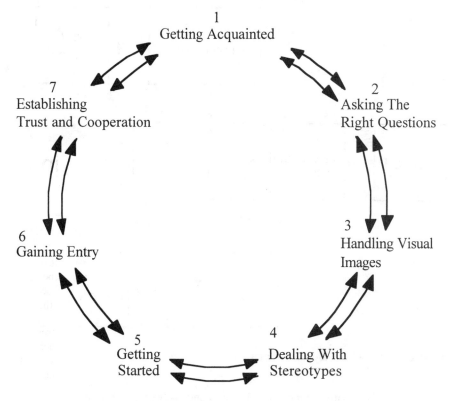

1
Getting Acquainted

7
Establishing
Trust and Cooperation

2
Asking The
Right Questions

6
Gaining Entry

3
Handling Visual
Images

5
Getting
Started

4
Dealing With
Stereotypes

FIGURE 4.1 **The Seven-Step Process (T.S.S.P.)**

In the process of getting acquainted, take care not to cause a communication break-down. Figure 4.2 shows two possible outcomes of a first encounter, with one leading to a dead end and the other resulting in more contacts.

When people from different cultures meet for the first time, they often approach the encounter with fear and anxiety. Both are wearing their cultural lenses and interpret events using their culture as a frame of reference. Visitors to the United States, for example, may interpret "hi" not as a greeting but a small joke. This is because a genuine greeting in their own cultures would last longer. In a greeting, some people go as far as asking about each other's health, work, and family members. When they ask, "How are you?" they genuinely want to know what is going on in the other person's life. It is not uncommon to hear a reply like, "Well, I would be all right if my wife had not fallen sick."

The first encounter is complicated further by nonverbal communication. Speech, styles of clothing, ways of shaking hands, eye contact or lack of it all tell something about the person we are encountering. If all goes well during this initial experience, fear and anxiety are relieved. Although the cultural lenses are still in place, they slowly give way to neutral ones.

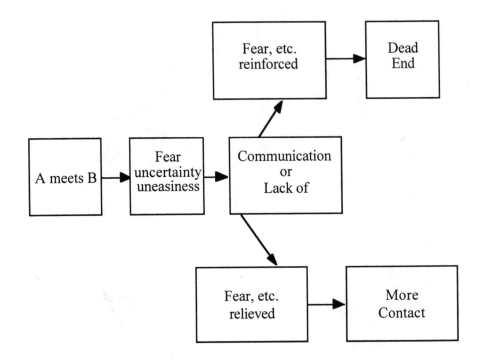

FIGURE 4.2 **The Cross-Cultural Encounter**

The second alternative that results in a dead end comes about because either one or both parties have been offended. The cultural lenses become thicker and the relationship gets terminated.

A major cause of the communication breakdown between members of different cultures is *ethnocentrism*. This term refers to the process of judging other cultures according to our own values and standards, instead of theirs. Although ethnocentrism has short-term benefits of instilling a sense of pride, well-being, and security, it inhibits our understanding of other people.

It is therefore very important that we deal with our ethnocentrism in preparation for the cross-cultural encounter. The following principles are a guide to acquiring a culturally neutral position.

1. Genuine interest
2. A sense of curiosity and appreciation
3. Empathy
4. Nonjudgmentality
5. Flexibility
6. Child-like learning mode

Genuine Interest

Many times we make the mistake of getting to know people from other cultures without any deeper motive than wanting to affirm beliefs in our own cultures. The prob-lem with this approach is that people from other cultures sense this attitude. As a result, even thicker walls than those that were initially in place are built and we end up worse off than we were before the meeting. Genuine interest is cultivated by a realization that culture is a relative concept. The best way of doing things is contingent on who we are dealing with. Cultures that do not have microwave ovens, dishwashers or electric shavers may interpret the use of these appliances as mere laziness. To dismiss such an attitude as backward is to deny the existence of differences. Another way to cultivate genuine interest in other cultures is to recognize that we can learn from them. We may, for example, find out that potatoes roasted in a charcoal oven taste better than those cooked in a microwave oven.

A Sense of Curiosity and Appreciation

In meeting other human beings and especially those whose cultures are different from our own, the quality, and not the quantity of those meetings contributes to a fruitful experience. Very often people meet others with no curiosity whatsoever. They leave the meeting with the same stock of knowledge they had before and experience little or no personal enrichment. Curiosity is not wrong as long as it is not aimed at debasing others. Someone wanting to know about another culture's eating habits could ask, "You eat snakes, don't you?" or "What are the common foods in your culture?" While the first question might prompt an answer like, "Yes, just like you eat snails," the second one will lead the speaker to list different foods which may or may not include snakes.

Most people do not appreciate behavior that does not resemble their own. Whether we want to admit it or not, people from other cultures do different things which may violate norms that we have held very dearly. Even small actions like cutting one's nails in front of others or wearing a shirt inside out can be sources of frustration for someone who has been raised to believe that such acts are wrong. One U.S. student once expressed frustration concerning foreigners who mix their clothing with those from the U.S. culture. Likewise, a foreigner to the U.S. culture found wearing a coat and tie with jeans very unappealing. In his culture, jeans are worn by children. According to this individual, if adults choose to wear children's items, they should not disguise them by adding adult clothing.

Although we may find certain acts unacceptable, we can learn to accept them as long as we appreciate others. A sense of appreciation comes from the realization that people do best what they have been taught. If we want them to see the world differently, we have to begin at their level and, with their cooperation, help them learn new ways.

Empathy

It is difficult to appreciate people from other cultures if we do not practice empathy; an ability to place ourselves in their position. Empathy is often confused with sympathy, which is usually an expression of pity or compassion for someone's state. Being empathetic is much more than a mental attitude or merely saying, "I can see that." While words can help someone express an empathetic attitude, the accompanying nonverbal communication is equally important. We should also be ready to admit that we actually do not fully know the experience of another person. It is, for example, less intimidating to ask someone from a tropical climate "What is the weather in your country like?" than saying "You must be enjoying this hot and humid weather since you come from the equatorial region." Not all equatorial regions are hot and humid since altitude modifies weather conditions. An empathetic attitude also demands that we listen attentively and pick up nonverbal cues. People from other cultures should be allowed to talk freely instead of simply responding to our communication agenda. If they are too shy or hesitant to start a conversation, we can probe and then let them choose what to talk about. We should not assume that what is painful or pleasant for us is viewed in the same way by others. For example, while some people openly discuss politics, religion, and social habits of their cultures, others may be more comfortable talking about neutral topics like the weather or technology.

Nonjudgmentality

If all of us were to take a test to measure our ability in judging other cultures, the majority would score very well. It is very easy to call this good and that bad without seriously considering the frame of reference that is being used to pass such judgments.

While a grasshopper eater might despise the person who eats crabs, both of these may consider eating pork an abomination. While it may be perfectly all right for a child to say parents' names in one culture, it is very impolite in another.

Very often, even without probing to find out why people behave the way they do, we rush to pass judgments about their behavior. On seeing a woman covered from head to toe, we may be tempted to say, "Look, she must be uncomfortable" or "Look at how oppressed that woman is!" At the same time, this particular woman may see our bare legs and say, "How indecent!" Believing in the concept of *cultural relativism* which en-ables us to judge other cultures by their standards instead of ours creates room for healthy cross-cultural relationships. Slowness in passing judgments about other cultures frees us from being locked up in our cultural cages and allows us to view the world differently.

Exercise

Describe a situation in which you have misjudged someone's behavior simply because he/she was from a different culture.

Flexibility

Working with people from other cultures demands a great deal of flexibility, an ability to change our behavior and courses of action according to the situation. If, for example, in the course of conversation, we discover that the people we are interacting with do not like to talk about a particular subject, we should not try to "push it down their throats." In such a situation, the subject could be changed easily, without tremendously interrupting the conversation flow. Care should be taken in choosing words with which to change the subject so that no one is left feeling embarrassed or guilty.

Flexibility also requires that we adjust to time and space usage in other cultures. When invited to eat at someone's house, the majority of Africans try to arrive a little late in order to give the hosts time to get ready. They also do not want to convey the image that they are starving. This behavior is contrary to the U.S. culture where punctuality at all times is the norm. People from these two cultures might find each other's behavior very odd and inconsiderate. When faced with such a situation, we may need to make a quick adjustment in order to avoid offending the other party. If puzzled about a certain behavior, we should always try to find a polite way of asking. One way of reducing tension is to ask other people from the same culture about expected behavior on particular occasions.

Child-Like Learning Mode

In order to make cross-cultural encounters successful, we can learn a lot from children's behavior. Having a child-like learning attitude is not the same thing as being childish. A child-like mind can be compared to an empty slate, ready to be covered with new meaning. Whereas a childish question might be, "Do you have houses where you come from?", a child-like question is "What kind of houses do you have where you come from?" The first type of question might arouse anger and prompt a cynic reply like, "No, we do not have houses. We all live in trees." The second one, on the other hand, expresses genuine interest and eagerness to learn. It might prompt an answer like, "We have different types of houses . . . ."

A major error that is often made is to assume that we already know a lot about the people we are encountering because we have read about their culture. Reading about another culture may provide us with a general picture but not the intricate rules of behavior. An author who is foreign to a culture may not succeed in capturing the real essence of a particular culture. The way words are arranged and emphasized highlights certain aspects of a culture and not others. Someone reporting about the Luo of Northern Uganda and Western Kenya, might spend more time describing the act of removing some of their lower teeth and the pain involved without paying much attention to the triumph and sense of beauty that come about afterwards. Likewise, someone else might write about rituals involving the birth of twins in many African cultures, without stressing the symbolic meaning of such rituals.

The second error that gets in the way of learning about other cultures comes from overgeneralization. Assuming that all Arabs, Africans, Asians, and Europeans are alike is a big mistake. Although we know that not all children from the same family are alike, we assume this to be true of people who share similar physical attributes or those who live in the same geographical region. This kind of assumption can spoil a cross-cultural experience right at the start. Although there are a few general characteristics that may describe a certain cluster of people, there may be more differences between subgroups than similarities. In case of doubt, it is polite to ask the people concerned to tell you how they would prefer to be treated. While a group of people from Nigeria may like to be called Africans on particular occasions, they may prefer to be known as Nigerians or Yoruba at other times.

Exercises

1. With other group members, discuss situations in which you are unwilling to compromise your own cultural values. Pay attention to instances where your own rigidity may conflict with other people's expectations.

2. Get into pairs and practice different styles of shaking hands in your culture. Talk about the meaning attached to each style and discuss your findings about this activity with the large group.

3. Divide into groups of 4 or 5 people. Each group needs to select a specific cultural group from any part of the world. Go to the library and find out all the available information about that group. Pay particular attention to the following:

   a. Way(s) of exchanging greetings.
   b. Forms of nonverbal communication and their meanings.
   c. Attitude toward life in general, authority and family in particular.

   Each small group should write a short summary on the particular culture studied and report the findings to the large group.

4. Imagine you are all delegates to the United Nations from different countries of the world. It is important that people get to know one another. Each member needs to introduce himself/herself to others using the following guidelines:

   a. Name(s), including nicknames
   b. The country you are from
   c. Your occupation
   d. Family background

   As the introduction is going on, the rest of the class should note the following:

   a. Information left out that could have contributed to knowing the person better.
   b. Forms of nonverbal communication whose meanings were not understood.
   c. What is admirable about the person who is making the introduction?

   After the introduction, all the members need to share their comments in an open discussion.

5. Individually, complete the following sentences:

   a. The country I would most like to visit is . . . .
   b. My greatest strength in relating to people from other cultures is . . . .
   c. My greatest weakness in relating to people from other cultures is . . . .

ASKING THE RIGHT QUESTIONS

Although some questions can be asked during the getting acquainted stage, care should be taken not to overwhelm others with questions about themselves and their culture too early in the interaction process. Too many questions at the beginning of the encounter can be off-putting. The person may feel that the exercise is more of an interrogation than an attempt at facilitating communication and understanding.

Asking questions is a fairly simple process but deciding on the right ones is harder. The following guidelines provide a strategy to address this dilemma.

1. Ask general questions first and specific ones later.
2. Make questions clear and simple.

3. Avoid sensitive questions.
4. Ask questions that are of interest to both of you.
5. Ask questions in a relaxed, nonthreatening manner.

General Questions First and Specific Ones Later

Starting off with general questions first puts the person from a different culture at ease. A question like "How was your trip?" is good to begin with. If the person answers, "Fine," then a little probing might help. Specific questions about the trip could be asked. They might include the airline used, the route followed, the times of departure and arrival, and the luggage handling. Depending on what kind of answers you get, further probing may be necessary or a very interesting conversation might evolve. During the discussion, pay attention to any indication of culture shock. The person might say, "All the way from London to New York, I never said a word." Instead of letting this pass, a question like, "Did you sit alone?" might prompt a long conversation about different cultural expectations. The person may have been surprised by the behavior of other passengers who did not talk to each other.

Once the conversation is progressing well, specific questions relating to family and country can be asked, as long as you are careful not to ask them in a derogatory fashion. Take time to respond appropriately to the answers given. If someone says, "I have a wife and nine children," it is very impolite to say, "You have all those children! My goodness, you have your hands full." The other person might be put off by such a remark and from then on, the conversation will become stilted and burdensome. A more neutral response might be, "How old are your children and what kinds of schools do they attend?"

Extra caution should also be exercised while handling questions of a political nature. A question like, "You have a dictatorial government, don't you?" might cause walls to be built between the communicating parties. The person might feel too insecure to criticize the government or the outside world might have a different picture from that of the indigenous people.

Sensitive Questions

What is considered sensitive in one culture could be common talk in another. Whereas talking about one's dead relatives might be easy in one culture, it may be taboo in another. While divorce is a common word in U.S. culture, it is not in many African and Asian societies. In a few cases where marriages between couples do not work out, the relationships are terminated without much talk about the subject. In these cultures, it is not very common to hear people talking about their "ex" husbands or wives.

Since we are not always sure about sensitive topics in cultures that are foreign to us, asking for clarification helps prevent problems. Be careful to respond appropriately when a question is answered. If, for example, someone says, "We don't talk about sex in public or on television" a reply like, "Don't be ridiculous, what is wrong with talking about it?" immediately builds defenses. A preferable response might be, "That is interesting. Why not?"

Questions of Interest

We often put off others by assuming that our favorite subject will interest them too. We also take it for granted that they understand what we are talking about and if they don't, then they should find out about it. Imagine a foreigner to U.S. culture who is involved in a conversation about football. Many people from other countries call what is known as soccer in the United States football. Besides confusing names, the visitors do not know the rules of the game. They may join in the conversation or even watch the game out of courtesy while they may be terribly bored. A genuine sense of inquiry into the interests of the visitor will eliminate boredom and a sense of hopelessness. If the person says, "I like bowling," answering "That's boring," gives an impression that this person has poor taste. A more positive approach could be, "Yes, bowling is also interesting. If you are interested in knowing the football rules, I will explain them to you. Or if you want, we can go to the bowling alley sometime either to watch or play. I will be glad to do whatever makes you comfortable."

Relaxed Manner

The ease with which cross-cultural encounters are handled is critical in creating a fruitful experience. The majority of people do not like to give away information about themselves, especially to someone who is not from their culture. Apart from simple mis-trust, there is a general fear that the information might be used against them in some way.

One person may not like to talk about circumcision as a ritual that marks the transition from childhood to adulthood for fear of being called "backward." Another may not want to talk about courting practices where the bridegroom-to-be has to chase the future bride and capture her as a sign of bravery for fear of being called "barbaric."

Recognizing that people from other cultures fear self-disclosure, extra effort should be made to calm their fears. If we want to learn from them, we need to create a conducive atmosphere that will facilitate the learning process. One way of being at ease is to curb our own fears of others. However composed we may try to be, a fearful state will always be recognized. The best way to overcome fear is to cultivate a belief in the goodness of others.

Exercises

Step One

Imagine you are meeting someone whose cultural expectations you are unfamiliar with; write down questions you might ask such a person on the following topics:

  a. Basic information about the person (e.g., name, occupation, age, family background, etc.).
  b. Country information (e.g., size, population, climate, type of government, etc.).
  c. Social customs (e.g., food, clothing, housing, family, religion, etc.).

Make sure that the questions are phrased in such a way as not to create barriers to communication.

Step Two

Get into groups of 4 to 5 people and discuss the questions developed in step one. Get a group leader to write down questions from the various group members, without repeating those that are similar.

Step Three

a. Each group leader is to write the questions on the board for everyone to see. With the help of the discussion leader, the questions should be grouped in categories of similar subject areas. The whole group should go through all the questions, discussing their strengths and weaknesses, until the best question is selected from each category.

b. Invite a guest or guests from a different culture to visit your class. Ask them to demonstrate how, using their culture as a reference point, they would ask the same questions as were asked in step one. Write down similarities and differences between these cultures and yours.

c. With the help of friends who speak more than one language, practice asking one particular question in as many other languages as you can. Spend some time discussing the experience of speaking several languages with other group members.

HANDLING VISUAL IMAGES

Expressions like "These are oriental colors" or "You have the body of a European" are not uncommon. Sometimes, we can visually picture subcultures and make statements like, "I could tell from the way he was dressed that he was a New Yorker" or as someone once remarked to me, "You have a Ugandan face." From experience, we have learned to associate certain body features, colors, clothing, and mannerisms with specific categories of people. While this categorization makes it easy for us to predict behavior, it can cause us to misjudge and misrepresent other people.

Since in many cases we do not know what people prefer to be associated with, we face the risk of either failing to compliment them or saying something that may offend them. While a statement like, "You look sexy" is all right in one culture, the same may be very embarrassing to someone from a different culture. People from all cultures strive to portray certain images and enjoy compliments. Rather than thinking, "Well, since I do not know what to say, I will not comment on their looks," practice dealing with images in a constructive way and minimize mistakes. When I had just arrived in the U.S., I remember paying someone a compliment by saying, "You have put on some weight; how wonderful." I was speaking from a culture that does not value excessive thinness. Since the woman did not express appreciation, I assumed she had not heard me and I elaborated by saying, "This summer you must have taken very good care of yourself. Your beautiful round cheeks show that you fed yourself adequately." She must have realized how naive I was because she simply smiled and moved away. She probably contacted "Weight Watchers" immediately! A few days later, I learned that being thin is a good thing in U.S. culture. I could have avoided hurting this person's feelings if only I had not assumed that my beauty standards are universal. The following principles can help in establishing a proper perspective of others:

1. Value neutrality.
2. Appreciate inner beauty.
3. Respect diversity.
4. Accept differences.

Value Neutrality

Being neutral about our own values when dealing with people from other cultures can help us avoid misunderstandings. Although cultural influences are so strong that they often get in the way of objectivity, trying constantly to be open-minded can be of great help. Steps to developing a value-neutral personality include: recognizing our biases and confronting them instead of suppressing them; seeing beauty in things that appear unfamiliar; and developing a high sense of self-esteem.

Appreciate Inner Beauty

Dealing with images that are unfamiliar to our cultural setting is quite a challenge and needs to be approached skillfully. Instead of looking at certain features, for example and concluding that a person is ugly, we could look for other beautiful features such as personality. Before concluding that a person is ugly, we need to recognize that beauty standards are relative. What we might call ugly by our cultural standards might be the source of beauty in the other person's culture. Recognizing sources of beauty other than visual ones increases our ability to use our sensory-perceptive skills.

Respect Diversity

Just as there is great diversity among the plant and animal kingdoms, the same is true for human beings. Although diversity can sometimes be a threat to unity, it also has the potential of creating greater harmony among human beings. If diversity is seen as a source of strength because it offers variety, then qualities that are unique to particular groups can be used for the benefit of the whole group. Just as different colors and shapes complement each other to make a good piece of artwork, diversity among people can be seen the same way. The following poem will aid in implementing this principle.

> A Bouquet of Flowers
>
> Life is like a bouquet of flowers
> If we claim it as truly ours
> It is full of wonder
> If we look here and yonder
> There is a purpose for all
> When we dare hear the call
> It's no mistake that we all differ
> For therein lies hope for sure

Hope that we indeed are free
And comfortable to the fullest degree
Free to add that other dimension
That liberates the soul from tension
Free to add that one other thread
On which we can tread
Free to add that one other grain
Which makes all others shine
A bouquet of flowers is what we are
Whose petals are seen from far

(Kabagarama, 1996)

Accept Differences

Accepting differences is based on an ability to respect diversity. Sometimes cultural differences are so pronounced that there is no apparent commonality between particular groups of people. This situation can best be illustrated by foods eaten in different cultures. In extreme cases where respect for differences may not be possible, mere acceptance may ease tension that could result from an attempt to move others to our side through force. We can successfully offer our alternative view after winning their trust and cooperation.

Exercises

1. Discuss images of beauty in your culture that are presented through television. Compare and contrast such images with the traditional ones. How have beauty standards changed over the course of time within your own culture?

2. List different types of costumes in your culture and the occasions that they are associated with. What do you like/dislike about these particular costumes?

3. Think of five different cultural groups.

    a. What traits do you admire in each of the groups?
    b. Which traits do you dislike in each of the groups?
    c. Why do you like the traits you said you like in certain groups and why do you dislike other traits?
    d. What traits do you think or have heard other cultural groups like in you? Which ones do they dislike?

4. Get into small groups of 4 to 5 people and discuss possible ways of developing and showing an appreciation for people who are different from you. Share these strategies with the large group.

5. Select five members of the group and let each one find a foreign costume to wear. Each of the five should appear before the large group in the costume for 3-5 minutes. The rest of the members should write down their feelings about the people in the costumes. Pay attention to the following:

a. Does the image arouse feelings of admiration or otherwise?
b. Do these people look intelligent, poor, foolish, dignified, etc.?

Why do you feel the way you do about a particular image?

6. If you had any negative feelings about a particular image or images, think of ways to overcome such feelings. Share your strategies with other members of your group and get additional advice from them.

DEALING WITH STEREOTYPES

According to Allport,[1] a *stereotype* is an exaggerated belief associated with a category (a group of people, such as a racial, ethnic, or religious group). A stereotype can either be positive or negative. Stereotypes can also be used in reference to subgroups from the same culture. In many societies where rules of patriarchy prevail for instance, the same trait may be positive for males and negative for females. An ambitious, rational, tough man may be admired for having businesslike traits while a woman with similar traits might be labeled pushy and unfeminine. In one culture, if a woman wears perfume, she is considered clean and elegant while a man who engages in the same behavior may be regarded as unmasculine.

Stereotypes very often get in the way of cross-cultural understanding. They are rooted in and help justify *prejudice* which is a tendency to negatively judge others based on personal characteristics, without any objective basis for making such a judgment. Prejudice often takes the form of overcategorization, which is a tendency to think of or react to everyone in a particular category in a fixed way.[2] We often make judgments about others based on characteristics such as skin color, hair color and texture, eye color, and body structure. We even go as far as categorizing others according to what society or culture they come from. Like ethnocentrism, negatively stereotyping those who are different from us makes us feel good about ourselves and our ways. However, this also prevents us from seeing the good in others. As a result, we fail to learn from those who are different from us and this limits knowledge acquisition. In the long run, our cultures get isolated from others and this hinders development.

Attempting to examine the stereotypes we hold about others is a key to building meaningful cross-cultural relationships. Without much thought, people make statements like, "I know those people are lazy by nature." In most cases, such conclusions are arrived at without much evidence. Guidelines to constructively dealing with stereotypes include the following:

1. Sincere self-examination.
2. Search for knowledge.
3. Practicing objectivity.

Sincere Self-Examination

Being honest about our views is necessary for understanding who we are and how we view the world around us. Many people want to face only the positive side of themselves because this makes them feel good. However, admitting to both the negative and positive aspects of our personality is essential for change and acquiring new knowledge. Someone might, for example say, "I am not prejudiced at all," or "How can I, of all people, be unfair to others and label them negatively?" However, in many cases it is one thing to wish we were free from bias and another to truly live by this principle.

Search for Knowledge

There is a Rutooro proverb which says, "Amagezi murro, bagwiiha nju eri," which means that knowledge is like fire because it is collected from somewhere else. Just as we turn to energy sources that give us fire, so we must turn to others in the process of knowledge acquisition. Another proverb states, "Akaana katabunga kangamba ngu nyi-nako nuwe achumba obunura" which means that a child that does not visit other homes believes that its mother is the only one who knows how to prepare delicious food. This proverb suggests that unless we are ready to seek knowledge from other cultures, we cannot fully see their strengths and our weaknesses. In searching for knowledge, we have to admit that our knowledge stock is insufficient and that we need more. We also have to admit that just as others want to learn from us, we too can learn a lot from them. This kind of attitude makes us free from prejudice and allows us to be sincere learners.

Practicing Objectivity

Overcoming stereotypic thinking requires an objective approach to life. Practicing rules of fairness helps in attaining objectivity. This can be successfully accomplished by setting up personal rules and adhering to them. One such rule could be, "I will not assume that people from other cultures are intellectually inferior" or "In my cross-cultural encounters, I will always make the first move and try to understand other people better" or "I will refrain from judging people solely on appearance." Such rules, if strictly followed, both in the public and private spheres of life, will over time shape an objective personality. Just as rules of hygiene become second nature when followed over and over again, so can those of objectivity.

Exercises

1. Make five rules for yourself that will help you handle cross-cultural encounters.

2. Close your eyes and picture the following types of people:

Americans (U.S.)	South Americans	Russians	Africans
Asians (in general)	Hispanic-Americans	Japanese	Arabs
Native-Americans	African-Americans	Europeans	Chinese
Asian-Americans	Caucasian-Americans	women	men

   a. Think of stereotypes that you associate with each group.
   b. What are the sources of these stereotypes?

3. Invite representatives from the groups listed in exercise number one or anyone who has visited or interacted at great length with them. Listen to their side of the story about those cultures.

4. Ask people who are foreign to your culture about the stereotypes they have of your culture and sources of such stereotypes.

GETTING STARTED

You may wonder why this stage is not the first one, since it deals with starting off. Handling cross-cultural encounters is not like reading a cookbook. There is background work that needs to be accomplished before we can move on to building healthy relationships. If, for example, we have not adequately handled visual images and stereotypes, it is difficult to get started.

Right from the beginning there is need to view someone from a different culture with a neutral lens. Thus, we can boldly move forward and proceed to interact without much fear of making mistakes. Even when mistakes do occur, they may not be detrimental to the relationship since we have shown sincere appreciation right from the start. We have also shown that we do not know everything about the other culture and are willing to learn. The following principles provide a guideline for getting started:

1. A positive outlook on life in general and on the encounter in particular.
2. Freedom from procrastination.
3. Ability to learn from mistakes.
4. Introspective interaction.

Positive Outlook

Believing in ourselves helps us achieve what we desire out of life. The same principle should help us attain healthy cross-cultural experiences. A high sense of self-esteem, coupled with a positive outlook on life, help us show the best side of ourselves. This image reduces fear, anxiety, and suspicion in the people we are interacting with. It also indirectly conveys a message that we are seeking to establish a relationship based on reciprocity, not exploitation. However, care should be taken not to confuse high self-esteem and pride. Whereas pride might convey a message of superiority, self-esteem shows self-confidence and a pleasant personality.

Freedom from Procrastination

Failure to establish a meaningful cross-cultural relationship can come from an inability to take the first step. When we procrastinate, we put off what could be done today until tomorrow. Take an example of someone who fails to approach a foreign student on a college/university campus, thinking they will do it later. This very behavior puts off people from cultures where a caring person is judged on the first encounter. It is during the initial stages of their stay that foreign students need the greatest amount of help in adjusting to a new setting. They will not appreciate someone who waits to let them learn from their mistakes first and then tries to make friends with them once they are well-established.

The main reason people procrastinate is fear of taking risks. While dealing with people whose ways we do not fully comprehend, often this fear is unfounded. The worst that can happen is experiencing rejection or a cold shoulder. When this happens, we can try to assess the cause of such a response and start anew. Or we may ascertain that our friendship is not appreciated and it would be best for us not to insist.

Learning from Mistakes

"I blew it; I must be a fool," is a common expression of people who make mistakes. Self-blame is particularly intense when we do not know the cause of our mistake or how to rectify the situation. The good thing about mistakes is that we can learn from them and develop alternative modes of conduct. Mistakes made during cross-cultural interaction are particularly troubling because in many cases, we are ignorant of the standards against which we are being judged. An act as small as a handshake may either create a healthy relationship or may completely ruin it. A foreign student once com-plained about an outstanding university official: "He shook everyone's hand and when it came to my turn, he ignored me." While there is a possibility that failure to shake this particular student's hand was intentional, it is also possible that the university official got distracted or tired at this particular moment. On realizing this mistake, it would have been perfectly all right for the official to approach the student and admit the mistake. He could, for example, say, "I do not recall shaking your hand" and offer his hand. When this is done well, with a good sense of humor, the end results are very rewarding to both.

Introspective Interaction

Although cultural habits can be described in books, experience is the best teacher. Very often, we fail to learn about other cultures because of engaging in superficial conversations. Introspective interaction requires that the communicating parties go below the surface to uncover what words mean in their cultural contexts. Someone may, for example, say, "I like your eyes." Instead of assuming that the person likes the eyes because of their color, one should be open to other possibilities. The size of the eyes, rather than their color might be the criterion on which judgments are made. Alternatively, the person may be impressed by the way the eyes are shaped and not by their size or color. The point to remember is that beauty standards and indeed the whole outlook on life are determined by different standards around the world.

Before coming to the U.S. a friend of mine told me that among other foods, peo-ple in this country eat hot dogs. My first reaction was, "What? I am not going to eat dogs. Whether hot or cold, dogs are dogs." Well, when I arrived in my new country, I was very suspicious of unfamiliar food, particularly if it was hot. With the passage of time and after being invited out to eat by friends, I realized that my fears were unjustified. I now enjoy hot dogs and they are actually the best dish for one of my children.

Exercises

1. Which food(s) from other cultures have initially put you off? Were you surprised when you actually tasted them?

2. a. For a week, record in a diary or journal all your encounters with people from other cultures. Upon meeting such people, try to make the first move at speaking to

them and record the experience, up to the smallest detail. Pay attention to what went right or wrong.

   b. Share the experiences with other members of the group.

3. With other group members, discuss ways of expressing happiness in your culture. Repeat the same exercise by discussing ways of expressing sorrow.

4. Imagine you are a visitor to another country; what things or places would you need most help finding?

5. Think of any embarrassing habits that you would hesitate sharing with someone else. Make a list of these and share them with other group members.

6. Identify subject areas that you would find embarrassing to discuss with someone from another culture. How can you go about overcoming such embarrassments?

7. Write an imaginary letter to someone who has never visited your country before.

   a. Make sure you tell this person as much information about your culture as possible. In the same letter, try to find out about their way of life.
   b. Swap the letters with other group members and let them describe what kind of impression they would have had about the writer's culture had they been from a different one.

GAINING ENTRY

Many people make a mistake of assuming that once a conversation is going well, they have absolutely succeeded in establishing healthy relationships. While this assumption may be partly true, there is a lot more that needs to be done in order to establish a firm relationship that is able to survive outside pressure.

   The following principles provide a guideline for successfully gaining entry into new cultures.

   1. Genuine interest.
   2. Good listening skills.
   3. Boundless generosity.
   4. Ability to give compliments.

Genuine Interest

When establishing any kind of relationship, people usually ask the question, "Is this person really interested in me?" Underlying this question is a fear of being exploited or taken for granted. When we feel that others are genuinely interested in us for who we are and not what they can get from us, there is a sense of relief and trust. However, if we feel that we are taken for granted or even despised, mistrust develops which often leads to hostility. Showing profound interest in someone from another culture cultivates trust, which is a key ingredient in establishing a firm, long-lasting, and meaningful relationship. Success at this benefits members of both cultures and creates a model for future generations.

Genuine interest is established through the development of an open mind. We have to be prepared to learn other ways of going about our daily business should an opportunity arise. If we are able to see the good in others, that is the starting point. We can practice this behavior by telling ourselves that as human beings we have a common bond and share the same destiny. Further, by practicing speculative imagination, we are able to picture others living fully productive lives in circumstances that are different from ours. Speculative imagination can be cultivated by telling ourselves that there are other methods of carrying on daily routines. We can, for example, picture the food we eat, the clothes we wear, the houses we live in and convince ourselves that other people around the world have alternatives to these things and that they are not necessarily of inferior quality.

Good Listening Skills

A good listener is able to catch both verbal and nonverbal cues. This trait is particularly essential in cross-cultural communication where nonverbal cues are often different or contradictory. A good listener also knows when the conversation is coming to an end or simply taking another direction.

People from different cultures pay attention differently. While U.S. people use their eyes a lot in showing attention or lack of it, most Africans move other body parts accordingly. Tilting the head so that the ear is in the direction of the speaker is one way of doing it. It is also common to clap hands once or touch the speaker as a sign that one is following the conversation and is in fact excited about it. Although there are differences like those just mentioned, all cultures have a way of judging an attentive listener. A preoccupation with other objects while the conversation is going on is a universal sign lack of attention.

There are many examples of behavior that may show that someone is not paying attention. Talking while looking at a computer program on the screen can demonstrate a lack of interest in the conversation. The speaker may react by saying "He (or she) was more interested in the machine than talking to me." Watching television while the conversation is going on may indicate that the conversation is less important than what is being discussed on television. In many cultures, nodding the head or interrupting with appropriate words shows that the other person is listening. There are situations when interrupting conversation is a sign of rudeness and others when failure to interrupt indicates a lack of interest. While most people do not mind being interrupted during conversations dealing with happy topics, they would rather be uninterrupted when discussing sad or serious subjects.

Boundless Generosity

When people have not been successful at cross-cultural encounters, they may be heard saying something like, "I did all I could to make her feel at home but she was so tense all the time." Whereas this may show a genuine sense of concern and despair on the part of the host, it is also blaming the visitor for failing to make a proper adjustment to a new cultural setting. Although it is possible that this particular person may be difficult to please, it is equally likely that the host did not try hard enough. Establishing firm cross-cultural relationships requires that we keep giving of our talents and resources. This does not mean that we spend up to our last penny in order to make the relationship work. It means offering assistance in situations where often it is assumed that people know what to do. Occasions involving food can be used as an illustration. When people who are new to a cultural setting are invited to a meal, they may expect assistance in serving. Extra care should be taken not to make them feel ignorant or helpless. However, it is better to assume that they need to know more about the food and how to serve it than to leave them scared to death and not knowing what to do. Someone who has never used chopsticks may feel awkward at the first encounter with such utensils, just as someone who has never eaten pizza may not know how to handle the stretching cheese. Talking about the food and how it is best handled may ease the tension that often accompanies such occasions. If the explanation is carried out with humor and respect, nobody's feelings will be hurt. If we choose to serve others, we should not assume that what we like to eat is equally appealing to them. While, for example, corn may be eaten with butter by some people, this is considered strange by others.

Ability to Give Compliments

Gaining entry into people's lives requires that we see the good in their ways and give compliments whenever possible. It is not hard to give compliments to people from similar cultural backgrounds since we know what standards to use. The tendency is usually not to offer compliments to those who are different for fear of offending them. This is a genuine concern since we may compliment them on a trait that they would prefer not to have. One may, for example, remark, "I like your hair." This statement could either pave the way to a wonderful relationship or may lead to cynicism. Cynicism arises if the person being complimented feels that the compliment was offered without much thought. The compliment could also be interpreted as, "I like your hair but I am glad it is not on my head."

Before offering compliments or refraining from them, it is best to find out about the person's interests and cultural values first. It is perfectly all right, for example to ask, "In your culture, how do women like to wear their hair?" The addressee may even go on to suggest that hers is not the ideal type. After such an explanation, a statement like, "But I like your hair," might prompt a reply like, "You sincerely do?" To her, it is a great discovery that other people find her hair beautiful.

Success at giving compliments with positive results is contingent on sincerity and honesty. An ability to see beauty in differences, and the desire to make people feel good about themselves are keys to establishing a positive attitude about those who are different from us.

Exercises

1. a. Choose a panel of 3 to 5 judges.
   b. While other group members practice complimenting each other, the judges should make note of any strengths and weaknesses shown.

2. With other members of the group, practice ways of inquiring into other people's well-being without making them feel uncomfortable.

3. List your strengths and weaknesses and identify ways in which these can either help or hinder you from understanding people whose cultures are different from your own.

4. Complete the following sentences:

   a. The areas of my life that I want people to know about are . . . .
   b. The areas of my life that I do not like people to know about are . . . .
   c. I like to learn about other cultures because . . . .
   d. I do not like to learn about other cultures because . . . .
   e. I get along with other people because . . . .
   f. I do not get along with other people because . . . .

ESTABLISHING TRUST AND COOPERATION

The final stage in creating healthy cross-cultural relationships involves estab-lishing trust and cooperation. Before this final stage, people may be merely getting along, not trusting one another to the extent of allowing self-disclosure. In order to establish an atmosphere of trust and cooperation, it is necessary to practice the following principles:

1. Availability whenever needed.
2. Ability to give and accept criticism.
3. Ability to be spontaneous.

Although adherence to these three principles is of paramount importance during this stage, they should also be present in the earlier stages.

Availability Whenever Needed

The saying "A friend in need is a friend indeed" best illustrates the importance of being available not only during good times but also in times of hardships. Most people, for example, believe that one cannot know a true friend except in times of trouble. It is during such moments that they feel most vulnerable and therefore need a lot of help. Opting to "give someone space" during hard times only serves to build barriers. It is indeed very difficult to know how to act in times of trouble. People from different cultures, for example, act differently at the loss of a loved one. While some want to be left alone in order to go through the grieving process, others prefer to be surrounded by caring people. Times of happiness are equally confusing. Traditionally, among Africans, for example, wedding feasts were open to whoever wished to attend. Modern times have put such tremendous budget constraints on families that even Africans now send invitations to selected guests for weddings. However, if some uninvited guests decide to join in the feast, they are not turned away or looked at suspiciously. After all, it is not uncommon in a clan system for people to have relatives that they may never have met before. Care is usually taken not to turn away strangers for fear that they might be distant relatives who will go away complaining.

Ability to Give and Accept Criticism

"He criticized me and made me look like a fool" is a common expression of people who do not take criticism very well. Constructive criticism can lead to both individual and relationship maturity. When a person takes criticism positively, he/she might be heard saying, "Our relationship is so firm that we are able to criticize each other and laugh about it later." Both the person giving and the one receiving criticism have to be at the same level of understanding. If either is suspicious of the other's motives, it is wise to refrain from criticism.

"How do we engage in criticizing others whose ways are foreign to us?" you might ask. Opting to remain clear of offering and receiving criticism keeps a relationship from growing. Criticism serves the following functions: uncovering our mistakes; putting a balance on our personality so that we do not assume an "always correct" attitude; telling us that the person who offered the criticism cares about us; and providing alternative courses of action.

Attention should be given to the time and place of criticizing, the words used, the nonverbal communication accompanying the message and the time lag between the act and the criticism of it. Many people prefer to be told of their mistakes in private and at a time when they are relaxed. It would be fruitless, for example, to meet a foreign student friend running to class to take a test and tell the person of the previous day's mistake at the dinner hosted by the university provost. If it is a serious mistake such as wearing shoes in a home where shoes are not permitted, being told right there and then might be appreciated.

The epithets "silly" and "stupid" are offensive in many cultures. Whereas among the U.S. people, it is common to hear people who love each other saying "you're silly" and laughing about it, other people might end up in a serious fight. It is therefore wise to use neutral words when offering criticism to someone whose culture we are unfamiliar with. Instead of saying, "Yesterday you looked silly in that dress," it might be better to say, "In this culture, people usually wear the dress like the one you had on yesterday to church or weddings. We are more casual at birthday parties." This kind of approach to the problem might prompt a response like, "What do you mean by casual?" At this stage, a more detailed explanation of the dress code might follow.

When giving and receiving criticism, it is important to pay attention to nonverbal cues. In most cases, the words are said very well but the accompanying gestures might be condescending. It is, for example, all right to say, "No, thank you. I will not taste this dish." However, it is terribly embarrassing if these words are accompanied by an expression of disgust. Criticism that is offered with a spirit of consideration and respect for others is usually taken well.

Ability to Be Spontaneous

Rigid thought and action patterns get in the way of building trust. Success at cross-cultural understanding requires that we show our true colors and refrain from wearing masks. Although such masks may have served as a prevention against vulnerability during the early stages, they should be removed to give way to spontaneity. Although U.S. people might find it easy to be spontaneous because of the value placed on informality, their strict attitude toward the management of time and adherence to schedules gets in the way. Most people like to "drop by" at a friend's house any time they feel like doing so. In fact, calling ahead of time, especially if it is a casual visit, might suggest that the relationship is not deep enough. It might also indicate that the person who is calling wants to be given special attention.

Rules regarding spontaneity are different for each cultural group. We have to develop a flexible attitude and be willing to sacrifice time and some of our privacy. Words that are used can either help establish trust or create barriers between people. At the ringing of the telephone, instead of saying, "What's up?" a response like, "I'm glad you called; what news do you have?" sounds better. The first response is too abrupt and might scare the person off. It almost suggests that there is an emergency situation which demands immediate attention, and after attending to the situation, there is no need for further conversation. This is not a good impression to give especially if you want to establish a firm relationship. What if the person just called to chat? The response is not conducive to chatting. If anything, it might give the impression that the caller is wrong for intruding. The second response creates room for discussing both major and minor items. The person might feel free enough to talk about personal issues like health problems, general business topics, or simply to chat and pass time.

Exercises

1. Practice carrying on a telephone conversation with someone from a different culture. Allow someone to listen to your conversation and give you feedback on your performance.

2. With other group members, list behaviors and actions that help build trust.

3. Imagine that you are all high-ranking government officials. You want to open up business transactions with another country. Discuss the steps you need to take in establishing trust and cooperation with your counterparts in that country.

4. You are stuck in an elevator with someone from another culture. The elevator will take several hours to repair, so it is necessary that you establish a good relationship with the person who is stuck with you. Discuss ways of winning this person's trust and cooperation.

5. a. Get a few volunteers from the group. Cover their faces and allow them to describe what it feels like to find themselves in a helpless situation.
   b. With all the members participating, discuss ways of expressing care and concern for the people who could not see so as to enable them to trust you.
   c. Discuss the appropriate responses that the people whose faces are covered need to exhibit in order to obtain maximum cooperation from their helpers.

ENDNOTES

1. Gordon W. Allport, *The Nature of Prejudice* (New York: Addison-Wesley, 1954).
2. John Farley, *Majority-Minority Relations* (Englewood Cliffs: Prentice-Hall, 1988).

► **5**

What Organizational Leaders Can Do to Foster Cross-Cultural Understanding

NATURE OF ORGANIZATIONS

The discussion in chapter one pointed out the changing nature of work relations. With increasing cultural diversity in the workplace, organizations need to respond favorably in order for them to remain effective.

Organizations are social structures created by individuals to support a collaborative pursuit of specific goals. As such, they have to define and redefine objectives, induce participants to contribute services, control and coordinate effort, gather resources from the environment, dispense services and products, train, replace participants, and maintain relations with neighbors. Such structures are not mere contexts influencing activities of individual actors, but actors in their own right. They are corporate persons, who are responsible for their actions.[1]

Some scholars have conceptualized organizations as *rational, natural,* and *open* systems. As rational entities, they are purposefully set up to pursue specific goals and have a deliberately-constructed formal structure. Being natural systems, they attend to their needs in an effort to survive and as open systems, they have interdependent activities with the outside environment from which they draw personnel and resources. In summary, organizations are constructed or enacted systems that must satisfy demands of members, owners, and constituents.[2]

It is imperative therefore, that in order for organizations to survive in a climate of tremendous internal and external change, they have to implement changes in strategy, structure, process and culture. This process requires a state of readiness in the members' behavior, attitudes, and intentions.[3]

ORGANIZATIONS AND CULTURAL DIVERSITY

These days "managing diversity" is becoming a corporate catchword due to a realization that in order to survive, organizations have to learn to operate under a climate of cultural diversity. In order for them to remain competitive, they need to capture the diverse talent. The manager who learns how to do this will be as indispensable to corporate management as working capital.[4] This is a task that demands investing a large amount of resources and energy, given that many organizations have been, for centuries, operating under the assumptions of a monoculture. As McGehee reiterates, much of the socialization process has been designed to make the U.S. people common-denominator citizens. If people read similar literature, speak the same language, then they would become alike, hold similar values, and create a unified society. There has been a tendency to be uncomfortable with difference. Talking about differences has not been encouraged. It has almost been seen as talking about a deficiency.[5] Proponents of cultural diversity argue, on the other hand, that the socialization process that expects people who hold diverse cultural values to be alike is too discriminatory and difficult to be achieved. They argue, further, that a process which destroys parts of some citizens is inequitable. Instead, focus should be on enriching each other by retaining and sharing differences, thereby learning to like one another, without becoming alike.[6]

In order for work organizations to remain effective, they have to pay particular attention to factors such as race, ethnicity, gender, and how these relate to individuals' perceptions and personality. Because employees join organizations after having been socialized in different cultural contexts, their values influence the nature and behavior of such organizations. They affect the supervisory relationship, perception of fairness, decision-making style, nature of political behavior, formal and informal networks, inter-group processes, and response to stress. If, for example, an individual is from a culture where authority is based on age and experience, joins an organization where skills and academic achievement are key variables in determining seniority, such an individual may experience a clash in values. This may result in unhappiness, conflict, confusion over expectations, alienation, poor mental and physical health, and poor performance. In the long run, this affects the overall productivity of the entire organization. The figure below illustrates the relationship between culture and organizational effectiveness.

Studies have observed that women and minorities' experiences in work organizations is different from that of white males. Over the past twenty years, research has found that in many organizations, women and minorities can only succeed to a certain level in the corporate hierarchy, beyond which there is a glass ceiling which blocks further development.[7] Due to such past discriminatory behavior, women and minorities may join organizations expecting the worst in terms of harassment, hostility, isolation, prejudice, rejection, resentment, and scapegoating.[8] These expectations may heighten their sensitivity to injustice, thereby creating an atmosphere of unhealthy human relations, leading to poor morale, poor health, and low productivity for the entire organization.

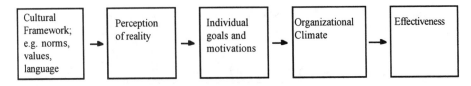

FIGURE 5.1 **The Impact of Culture on Organizational Effectiveness**

DIVERSITY AND EFFECTIVENESS

The discussion in this section of the book stresses the importance of recognizing diversity and utilizing it to the advantage and success of work organizations. Makower[9] asserts that the power of diversity lies in the different perspectives that employees bring to the decision-making process. Despite growing acknowledgment that diversity is critical to improving productivity, managing diversity does not come naturally to many managers or employees who have had little meaningful exposure to people outside their own racial, cultural, generational, or socio-economic circles. A strategy has to purposefully be designed to manage a diverse workforce and motivate all participants to achieve to their highest potential levels. It is therefore not enough to acknowledge that diversity exists but extra steps should be taken to design and implement those policies and programs that ensure that diversity is producing positive results.

Diversity need not be threatening, for if properly handled, people from a diverse background can lead to higher productivity, after all, they all contribute uniquely to the whole. In his study of insurance companies, Robert Miles[10] observed, that companies that were rated high in overall corporate social performance had a substantially higher number of women and minorities on their boards of directors than those that rated lower. His conclusion was that differences in values powerfully shape orientations that members of organizations have toward elements of the corporate social environment. They also influence the level of effectiveness in understanding and managing social and political contingencies affecting business operations. In order to be effective therefore, the organization needs to adopt its policies to the needs of a changing society. Sims and Dennehy[11] conclude that the extent to which American multiculturalism will succeed depends largely on the ways in which cultural differences among groups are reconciled and tension resolved.

ORGANIZATIONAL RESPONSE TO ENVIRONMENTAL PRESSURES

Although rigorous research is still lacking in organizational response to cultural diversity, some scholars have observed that current corporate structures do not promote diversity; in fact, they attempt to sabotage it.[12] This is the case despite scholars' warnings that in order to remain effective, organizations need to learn, unlearn and respond constructively to environmental changes. Leavitt[13] reiterates that organizational structure and performance is not only based on the initial resource mix and assortment. The creation of an organization is a continuing process and particularly fateful for the late stages of this process are the numbers and types of participants recruited in the earlier stages. Effective learning leads to greater ability in coping with problems. Growth in knowledge is important but such knowledge becomes obsolete as reality changes. Understanding involves both learning new knowledge while discarding that which is obsolete and misleading. Although unlearning is as crucial as learning new knowledge, Olsen and March[14] have observed that slow unlearning is a major weakness of organizations.

Organizational learning includes both processes by which organizations adjust themselves defensively to reality and by which knowledge is used offensively to improve relations between the organization and its environment. These strategies were demonstrated by Robert Miles'[15] outstanding research among the "Big Six" tobacco corporations. The study focused on their response to research linking smoking with cancer, thereby threatening their survival. Miles concluded that although each company adopted different strategies, including product innovation and diversification, they also took collective action such as creating the tobacco industry research committee, lobbying and establishing cancer research funds.

TIPS FOR LEADERS OF ORGANIZATIONS

In order to effectively manage a culturally-diverse workforce, leaders need to design and follow a clear strategy. Just as much attention should be paid to this aspect of organizational operations as is devoted to other areas such as financial management, market research and capital improvement. It is the leader who recognizes that culture has a strong influence on organizational effectiveness and designs rigorous methods of tapping into this particular resource, that will be able to get ahead in the next century. Investing in sophisticated technology is useful but so is tapping into the human potential that gives rise to inventing and using technology. A six-part model is presented and explained to help leaders get beyond recognizing the presence of cultural diversity to utilizing it to the best advantage of the organization. The model, LIVECC, presented in Figure 5.2 has the following components: Learn, Invest, Value, Experience, Commit and Change. Culture is shown in the center, being impacted by and in return, impacting each one of the six areas. Further, arrows linking the various parts of the model point in each direction, showing the interconnectedness between the parts. Implied in this is the idea that all the parts are linked and a change in one affects all of them.

LEARN

Ability to effectively manage a culturally-diverse workforce comes from a willingness to learn new ideas. Cultures differ in the way they conceptualize, organize and interpret both their material and non-material worlds. Differences range from seemingly simple things such as perceptions of beauty, elegance, clothing style, food habits to more complex issues such as religion and spirituality, perception of right and wrong, work ethic, allocation and use of time, interpersonal relations, power and authority and what it means to be a successful individual.

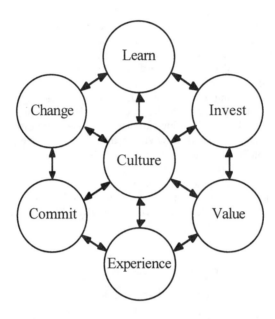

FIGURE 5.2 **The LIVECC Model of Organizational Effectiveness**

Learning about other cultures can take place in formal settings such as courses, and day-to-day, informal contacts. Leaders need to design programs for formal learning and also create an atmosphere where members of the organization are willing to learn from one another, informally. Dinners, sports events, home visits are excellent ways to provide a conducive atmosphere to learning. In order for the learning process to leave a long-lasting effect, it has to be carried out in an atmosphere of respect.

INVEST

Cultural learning does not take place automatically. Just as the organization invests in capital, technology and buildings, there is need to invest time, money and human power to promote cross-cultural understanding. Learning organizational operations such as technology takes a tremendous amount of time. Cultural learning should be handled in a similar manner. How much training is enough? As much training should be offered until members of the organization feel confident about handling cross-cultural encounters. They should reach a stage where they can realize the benefits of learning about other cultures in their private and public lives. Cultural learning can be compared to language learning. A language is not mastered until one uses it to better himself or herself. When this stage is reached, then the search for more knowledge starts to come from within the individual instead of responding to external pressures.

In order for the organization to realize its objectives, there is need to invest money and manpower to provide the know-how. Computer specialists, engineers and other types of experts need special training and an adequate reward system in order for them to perform their duties effectively. The same should be true in the area of cross-cultural understanding. Well-qualified experts need to be hired so that they can facilitate the learning process and also resolve any conflict that may arise because people differ in their cultural orientations.

VALUE

In order for any information or product to take firm roots, it has to be valued. It is important to value information and people from different cultures. They should be regarded as a necessary component for the organization's success. When the leaders demonstrate that they value cultural learning, this attitude will trickle down to other members of the organization. However, if leadership is removed from it and promotes it for others and not for themselves, their motives might be suspect. Employees might ask, "Well, if all this is good for us, then why don't our bosses like it?" This type of uneasiness may result in a "don't care" attitude or one where the minority cultures are regarded as inferior—cultures to hear about but not to take seriously. During this period of globalization, such an attitude may result in monetary and job losses and incompetence in a global economy.

EXPERIENCE

Learning about other cultures goes beyond book knowledge to actually incorporating what is learned in day-to-day organizational operations. One of the most effective ways of experiencing other cultures is to have a diverse workforce. Efforts should be made not only to recruit employees from a variety of cultures but to also create an atmosphere where they are accepted and valued. Equally important is the need for such individuals to be included in the management team. If some lack the skills that the organization needs, there is need to invest in them by offering special training in areas that are lacking.

Besides recruiting more employees from underrepresented groups, members of the majority culture need immersion experiences into other cultures. A "buddy" system could be developed whereby individuals from different cultural backgrounds can form teams and learn from each other. The total organization can also experience cultural diversity through recognizing holidays, languages and other cultural traits of the populations represented.

COMMIT

Commitment to cultural diversity is demonstrated through learning, investing, valuing, and experiencing. However it goes beyond these elements by incorporating a time component. When the organization is committed to cross-cultural understanding, all aspects of it should be affected. All departments need to be involved in the process just as they do in budget issues, employee recruitment and other functions. The organizational climate should be affected in such a way that the programs would stay, irrespective of who is in the position of leadership. Promoting cultural diversity should be stressed in the organization's rules and procedures, handbooks and newsletters.

CHANGE

The final component of organizational effectiveness through cultural diversity is the ability to bring about change. Implied in change is the idea that the organization moves from one state to another. When the other five components are implemented successfully, change becomes obvious. However, in order for remarkable change to take place, the organization has to have in place an evaluation tool with which to measure success. Short-term and long-term goals and objectives should be set up and after a period of time, an evaluation should be conducted, using a valid and reliable instrument. If the members' behavior, attitudes and belief system are changed due to exposure to cultural programs, then obviously, the organization has moved to another level of functioning. If, however, very little or no impact has been made, then there is need to revise the whole program and start anew.

DISCUSSION TOPICS

1. Discuss possible reasons why work organizations in the U.S. have been slow in responding to the needs of a culturally-diverse workforce?
2. What are the costs to work organizations and to the nation of failing to address needs of a culturally-diverse workforce?

EXERCISE

1. Imagine you are a leader of a work organization. Design a cultural learning program for your organization. Discuss any obstacles that you would encounter.

ENDNOTES

1. James Coleman, *Power and the Structure of Society* (New York: W. W. Norton and Co., Inc., 1974).
2. Richard Scott, *Organizations: Rational, Natural and Open Systems* (Englewood Cliffs, New Jersey: Prentice-Hall, 1992).
3. Achilles A. Armenakis, Stanley A. Harris and Kevin W. Mossholder, "Creating Readiness for Organizational Change," *Human Relations 46* (1993), 681–703.
4. Audrey Edwards, "The Enlightened Manager: How to Treat Your Employees Fairly," *Working Woman 16* (1991), 45–47.
5. Audrey Edwards, Ibid (1991), 46.
6. Larry McGehee, "Coming to Terms with the Multiculturalists," *The Civic Arts Review 4* (1991), 3–4.

7. Joy P. Cunningham, "Fostering Advancement for Women and Minorities," *Public Management* (1992), 21–25.

8. Jan C. Bird, "Respecting Individual and Cultural Differences: A Prescription for Effective Supervision," *FBI Law Enforcement Bulletin* (1993), 18–20.

9. Joel Makower, "Managing Diversity in the Workplace," *Business and Society Review* (1995), 48–54.

10. Robert Miles, *Managing the Corporate Social Environment* (Englewood Cliffs, New Jersey: Prentice-Hall, 1987).

11. Ronald A. Sims and Robert Dennehy, *Diversity and Differences in Organizations; An Agenda for Answers and Questions* (Westport, Connecticut: Quorum Books, 1993), 461.

12. Gary Heil, "Learning to Love 'Weird'; Creating an Infrastructure for Diversity," *Diversity and Differences in Organizations: An Agenda for Answers and Questions,* eds. Ronald R. Sims and Robert Dennehy (Westport, Connecticut: Quorum Books, 1993).

13. Harold J. Leavitt, "Applied Organizational Change in Industry: Structural, Technological and Humanistic Approaches," *Handbook of Organizations*, ed. James G. March (Chicago: Rand McNally, 1965), 1144–1170.

14. James G. March and Johan P. Olsen, *Ambiguity and Choice in Organizations* (Bergen: Universitet Sforlaget, 1976).

15. Robert Miles, *Coffin Nails and Corporate Strategies* (Englewood Cliffs, New Jersey: Prentice-Hall, 1982).

Bibliography

Adler, Nancy J. International Dimensions of Organizational Behavior. Boston: Kent Publishing Co., 1986

Albright, Alice Chu and Lori Austin. Moving and Living Abroad. New York: Hippocre Books, 1986.

Allport, Gordon W. The Nature of Prejudice. New York: Addison-Wesley, 1954.

American Council of Education, "Minority Changes Hold Major Implications for U.S.," Higher Education and National Affairs, 1984.

Armenakis, Achilles A., Stanley A. Harris and Kevin W. Mossholder. "Creating Readiness for Organizational Change," Human Relations 46 (1993) 681–703.

Bartlett, Christopher and Sumantra Ghoshal. Managing Across Borders: The Transnational Solution. Cambridge: Harvard Business School Press, 1989.

Batchelder, Donald and Elizabeth Warner. Beyond Experience: An Experiential Ap-proach to Cross-Cultural Education. Brattleboro: The Experiment Press, 1971.

Bauer, E. A. "Personal Space: A Study of Blacks and Whites," Sociometry 36 (1973) 402–408.

Baxter, J. "Interpersonal Spacing in Natural Settings," Sociometry 33 (1970) 444–456.

Bellah, R., R. Madsen, W. Sullivan, A. Swindler, and S. Tipton. Habits of the Heart: Individualism and Commitment in American Life. New York: Harper & Row, 1985.

Bennett, Christine I. Comprehensive Multicultural Education. Boston: Allyn and Bacon, 1990.

Berger, John. Ways of Seeing. New York: Penguin Books, 1987.

Bird, Jan C. "Respecting Individual and Cultural Differences: A Prescription for Effective Supervision," FBI Law Enforcement Bulletin (1993) 18–20.

Bornlund, Dean C. Communicative Styles of Japanese and Americans: Images and Realities. Belmont: Wadsworth Publishing, 1989.

Bornlund, Dean C. Public and Private Self in Japan and the United States: Communicative Styles of Two Cultures. Yarmouth: Intercultural Press, 1975.

Brislin, Richard. Cross-Cultural Encounters. New York: Pergamon, 1981.

Brown, Lester. State of the World: 1989. New York: W. W. Norton Company, Inc., 1989.

Bruneau, T. J. "Communicative Silences: Forms and Functions," Journal of Communication 56 (1973) 17–46.

Casmir, Fred L. Intercultural and International Communication. Washinton, D.C.: University of America Press, 1978.

Casse, Pierre and Swinder Deol. Managing Intercultural Negotiations: Guidelines for Trainers and Negotiators. Washington, D.C.: Sietar, 1985.

Coleman, James. Power and the Structure of Society. New York: W. W. Norton and Co., Inc., 1974.
Condon, John. "So Near the United States: Notes on Communication Between Mexicans and North Americans," Intercultural Communication: A Reader, eds. Samovar, Larry A. and Porter, Richard E. (Belmont: Wadsworth Publishing Company, 1991) 106–112.
Condon, John and Fathi Yousef. An Introduction to Intercultural Communications. Indianapolis: Bobbs Merrill, 1975.
Cooley, Charles H. Human Nature and the Social Order. New York: Scribners, 1902–1904.
Culick, S. The East and West: A Study of Their Psychic and Cultural Characteristics. Ruthland: Charles Turtle, 1962.
Cunningham, Joy P. "Fostering Advancement for Women and Minorities," Public Management (1992) 21–25.
Curt, C. and J. Nine. "Hispanic-Anglo Conflicts in Non-Verbal Communication," Perspectives Pedagogicas, ed. Isidora Albino. San Juan, Puerto Rico: Universidad de Puerto Rico, 1983.
Dali, Samuel. Personal Interview. McPherson College, 1991.
Dean, L. M., F. N. Willis, and J. N. LaRocco. "Invasion of Personal Space as a Function of Age, Sex and Race," Psychological Reports 38, (1976) 959–965.
Devita, Carol. The United States at Mid-Decade. Washington, D.C.: Population Bulletin, vol. 50, no. 4, 1996.
Dodd, Carley H. Dynamics of Intercultural Communication. Dubuque, Wm. C. Brown, 1991.
Dodd, Carley H. and Frank F. Montalvo. Intercultural Skills for Multicultural Societies. Washington, D.C.: Sietar, 1987.
Doz, Yves and C. K. Prahalad. The Multinational Mission: Balancing Local Demands and Global Vision. New York: Free Press, 1987.
Edwards, Audrey. "The Enlightened Manager: How to Treat Your Employees Fairly," Working Woman 16 (1991) 45–47.
Evans, Paul, Yves Doz, and Andre Laurent. Human Resource Management in International Firms: Change, Globalization and Innovation. New York: St. Martin's Press, 1990.
Farley, John. Majority-Minority Relations. Englewood Cliffs: Prentice-Hall, 1988.
Farley, John E. Sociology. Englewood Cliffs: Prentice-Hall, 1990.
Freeman, Robert E. Promising Practices in Global Education. New York: National Council of Foreign Language and International Studies, 1986.
Furnham, Adrian and Stephen Bochner. Culture Shock. New York: Methnen, 1986.
Gang, Philip S. Rethinking Education. Atlanta: Dagaz Press, 1989.
Geert, Hofstede. Culture's Consequences: International Differences in Work-Related Values. Newbury Park: Sage Publications, Inc., 1984.
Giddens, Anthony. Introduction to Sociology. New York: W. W. Norton & Company, 1996.
Gordimer, Nadine. The Essential Gesture. New York: Alfred A. Knopf, Inc., 1988.
Gordon, Raymond. Living in Latin America: A Case Study in Cross-Cultural Communication. Spokie: National Textbook Co., 1976.
Green, Madeleine. Minorities on Campus. Washington, D.C.: American Council on Education, 1989.
Gudykunst, W. B. Bridging Differences: Effective Intergroup Communication. Newbury Park: Sage Publications, 1991.
Gudykunst, W. B. and Y. Y. Kim. Communicating with Strangers. New York: Random House, 1984.
Hall, E. T. Beyond Culture. New York: Doubleday, 1976.
Hall, E. T. The Hidden Dimension. New York: Doubleday, 1966.
Hall, Edward T. The Dance of Life: The Other Dimension of Time. New York: Anchor Press/Doubleday, 1983.

Hammond, Samuel H. "Arband Moslem Rhetorical Theory," Central States Speech Journal (1963) 97–102.

Harris, Philip and Robert Moran. Managing Cultural Differences. Houston: Gulf Publishing Co, 1991.

Harrison, Paul C. The Drama of Nommo. New York: Grove, 1972.

Haviland, William A. Cultural Anthropology. New York: Holt, Rinehart and Winston, 1987.

Heil, Gary. "Learning to Love 'Weird'; Creating an Infrastructure for Diversity," Diversity and Differences in Organizations: An Agenda for Answers and Questions, eds. Ronald R. Sims and Robert Dennehy. Westport, Connecticut: Quorum Books, 1993.

Hillard, A. "Alternatives to IQ Testing: An Approach to the Identification of Gifted Minority Children." Final Report to the California State Department of Education, 1976.

Joijer, Harry. "Cultural Implications of Some Navajo Linguistic Categories," Language in Culture and Society, ed. Hymes, D. (New York: Harper & Row, 1964) 142–160.

Hopmann, Terrence P. "Communication and Bargaining in International Diplomacy," Intercultural and International Communication, ed. Casmir, Fred. (Washington, D.C.: University of America Press, 1978) 579–613.

Howard, Michael C. Contemporary Cultural Anthropology. Glenview: Scott, Foresman and Company, 1989.

Hsu, L. K. Francis. "The Cultural Problem of the Cultural Anthropologist," American Anthropologist 81 (1979) 58.

Karmin, Monroe. "Economic Outlook: My House Is Your House," U.S. News and World Report, 1988.

Keffler, Jean B. "Managing Changing Organizations: Don't Stop Communicating." Minneapolis: Paper delivered at the National Assessment Conference, 1991.

Kim, Young Yun and W. B. Gundykunst. Theories in Intercultural Communication. Newbury Park: Sage Publications, 1988.

Kennedy, John F. A Nation of Immigrants. New York: Harper and Row, 1964.

Kirdar, Üner. Change: Threat or Opportunity? New York: United Nations Publications, 1992.

Kochman, Thomas. Black and White Styles in Conflict. Chicago: The University of Chicago Press, 1981.

Lanier, Raymond A. Living in the USA. Yarmouth: Intercultural Press, 1988.

Leavitt, Harold J. "Applied Organizational Change in Industry: Structural, Tech-nological and Humanistic Approaches," Handbook of Organizations, ed. James G. March. (Chicago: Rand McNally, 1965) 1144–1170.

Lebra, T. S. Japanese Patterns of Behavior. Honolulu: The University Press of Hawaii, 1976.

Lengerman, Patricia M. and Ruth A. Wallace. Gender in America: Social Control and Social Change. Englewood Cliffs: Prentice-Hall, 1985.

March, James G. and Johan P. Olsen. Ambiguity and Choice in Organizations. Bergen: Universitet Sforlaget, 1976.

Makower, Joel. "Managing Diversity in the Workplace," Business and Society Review. (1995) 48–54.

Marshall, Charlotte. Culture Shock: What It Is and What to Do About It. San Francisco: American Friends Service Committee, 1990.

Martin, Philip and Elizabeth Midgley. Immigration to the United States: Journey to an Uncertain Destination. Washington, D.C.: Population Bulletin, vol. 49, no. 2, 1994.

Mazrui, Ali A. and Toby K. Levine. The Africans. New York: Praeger, 1986.

McGehee, Larry. "Coming to Terms with the Multiculturalists," The Civic Arts Review 4. (1991) 3–4.

McKay, Virginia. Moving Abroad: A Guide to International Living. Wilmington: VLM Enterprises, 1982.

Mead, George H. Mind, Self and Other. Chicago: University of Chicago Press, 1962.

Mendenhall, Mark and Gary Oddou. International Human Resource Management. Boston: PWS-Kent Publishing Co., 1991.

Miles, Robert, Coffin Nails and Corporate Strategies. Englewood Cliffs, New Jersey: Prentice-Hall, 1982.

Miles, Robert. Managing the Corporate Social Environment. Englewood Cliffs, New Jersey: Prentice-Hall, 1987.

Miller, Gerald R. and Mark Steinberg. Between People: A New Analysis of Interpersonal Communication. Chicago: Science Research Associated, 1975.

Muller, R. New Genesis. New York: Doubleday and Company, 1990.

Murdock, George P. "Comparative Data on the Division of Labor by Sex," Social Forces, no. 15 (1935).

Naisbitt, John and Patricia Aburdene. Megatrends 2000. New York: William Morrow and Company, Inc., 1990.

O'Hare, William P. America's Minorities—The Demographics of Diversity. Washington, D.C.: Population Bulletin, vol. 47, no. 4, 1994.

Olaniyan, Richard. African History and Culture. Lagos: Longman, 1982.

Paige, Michael R. Cross-cultural Orientation: New Conceptualizations and Applications. Washington, D.C.: University of America Press, 1986.

Parker, Woodrow M. and Charles C. Thomas. Consciouness-Raising: A Primer for Multicultural Counseling. Springfield: Charles C. Thomas, 1988.

Pederson, Paul. Handbook of Cross-cultural Counseling and Therapy. Greenwood: Greewood Press, 1985.

Perry, William. Forms of Intellectual and Ethical Development in the College Years. New York: Holt, Rinehart and Winston, 1970.

Piet-Pelon, Nancy J. and Barbara Hornby. In Another Dimension. Yarmouth: Intercultural Press, 1985.

Reischauer, E. The Japanese. Cambridge: Harvard University Press, 1977.

Reusch, Jurgen and Gregory Bateson. The Social Matrix of Psychiatry. New York: W. W. Norton, 1951.

Ruben, Brent and Richard Budd. Human Communication Handbook: Simulations and Games. Rochelle Park: Hyden Book Co., 1975.

Rumbaut, Rubén G. "Passages to America: Perspectives on the New Immigration," America at Century's End, ed. Wolfe, Alan. (Berkeley: University of California Press, 1991).

Samovar, Larry A. and Richard E. Porter. Intercultural Communication: A Reader. Belmont: Wadsworth Publishing Co., 1991.

Samuda, R. J. and A.Wolfgang. Intercultural Counseling and Assessment: Global Perspectives. Lewiston: Hogrefe, Inc., 1983.

Sapir, Edward. "The Status of Linguistics as a Science," The Selected Writings of Edward Sapir in Language, Culture and Personality, ed. Mandelbaum, David. (Berkeley: University of California Press, 1949) 160–166.

Schramm, Wilbur. The Science of Human Communication. New York: Basic Books, 1963.

Scott, Richard. Organizations: Rational, Natural and Open Systems. Englewood Cliffs, New Jersey: Prentice-Hall, 1992.

Shannon, Claude E. and Warren Weaver. The Mathematical Theory of Communication. Urbana: University of Illinois Press, 1964.

Shuter, Robert. "Non-Verbal Communication: Proxemics and Tactility in Latin America," Journal of Communication 26 (1976) 46–52.

Sikkema, Mildred and Agnes Niyekawa. Design for Cross-cultural Learning. Yarmouth: Intercultural Press, 1987.

Sims, Ronald A. and Robert Dennehy. Diversity and Differences in Organizations; An Agenda for Answers and Questions. Westport, Connecticut: Quorum Books, 1993.

Spradley, James P. and David W. McCurdy The Cultural Perspective. New York: John Wiley and Sons, Inc., 1975.

Stewart, Edward. American Cultural Patterns: A Cross-Cultural Perspective. Yarmouth: Intercultural Press, 1985.

Storti, Craig. The Art of Crossing Cultures. Yarmouth: Intercultural Press, 1989.

Sussman, N. and H. M. Rosenfeld. "Influence of Culture, Language and Sex on Conversational Distance," Journal of Personality and Social Psychology 42 (1982) 66–74.

Time, 1 March, 1989.

Torbiorn, Ingermar. Living Abroad. New York: John Wiley and Sons, 1982.

United Nations Population Division. World Population Prospects. New York: United Nations, 1991.

U.S. Bureau of the Census. Washington, D.C.: Census, 1990.

U.S. Bureau of the Census. Statistical Abstract of the United States. Washington, D.C.: Government Printing Office, 1992.

U.S. Bureau of the Census. Population Projections of the United States by Age, Sex and Hispanic Origin: 1993 to 2050. Washington, D.C.: Government Printing Office, 1993.

U.S. Immigration and Naturalization Service, Annual Reports. Washington, D.C.: Government Printing Office, 1960–77.

U.S. Immigration and Naturalization Service, Statistical Yearbooks. Washington, D.C.: Government Printing Office, 1978–89.

U.S. Immigration and Naturalization Service. Washington, D.C.: Statistical Year-book, 1993.

U.S. News and World Report, "Where the Tourists Go," February, 1990.

U.S. News and World Report, August 1, 1988.

Wattenberg, Ben J. "Tomorrow," U.S. News and World Report, 1989.

Wedge, Bryant. Foreign Visitors and How They See Us. New York: Van Nostrand, 1965.

Werkman, Sidney. Bringing Up Children Overseas: A Guide for Families. New York: Basic Books, 1977.

Wolfe, Alan. America at Century's End. Berkeley: University of California Press, 1991.

Wurzel, Jaime. Toward Multiculturalism. Yarmouth: Intercultural Press, 1989.

Zikopoulos, Marianthi. Open Doors 1988/1989: Report on International Education. Institute of International Education, 1989.

Zuckerman, Mortimer B. "What Should Make Bush Run Now," U.S. News and World Report, 1989.